CW00759059

# Be Careful
# What You
# Wish For
## From Cult to Occult

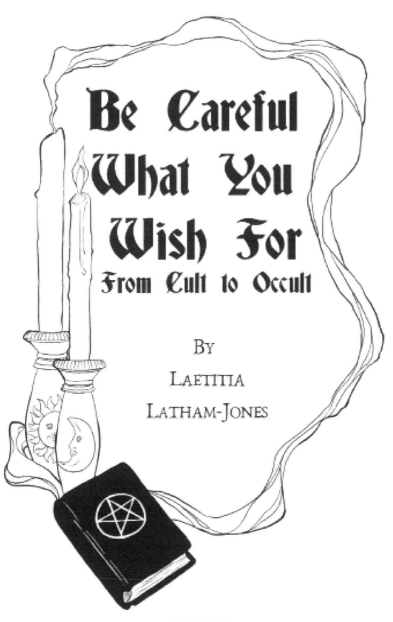

# Be Careful What You Wish For

## From Cult to Occult

By

Laetitia
Latham-Jones

Chicago, Illinois

Copyright © 2022 by Laetitia Latham-Jones. All rights reserved. No part of this book may be reproduced in any manner whatsoever without written permission from Crossed Crow Books, except in the case of brief quotations embodied in critical articles and reviews.

First Printing, 2022

ISBN 979-8-9856281-8-0
Library of Congress Control Number: 2022945937

Cover design by Wycke Malliway.
Typesetting by Wycke Malliway.
Edited by Rossa Crean.

Disclaimer: Crossed Crow Books, LLC does not participate in, endorse, or have any authority or responsibility concerning private business transactions between our authors and the public. Any internet references contained in this work were found to be valid during the time of publication, however, the publisher cannot guarantee that a specific reference will continue to be maintained. This book's material is not intended to diagnose, treat, cure, or prevent any disease, disorder, ailment, or any physical or psychological condition. The author, publisher, and its associates shall not be held liable for the reader's choices when approaching this book's material. The views and opinions expressed within this book are those of the author alone and do not necessarily reflect the views and opinions of the publisher.

Published by:
Crossed Crow Books, LLC
1407 W Morse Avenue
Chicago, IL 60626

Printed in the United States of America.

# Acknowledgements

*I would like to acknowledge and give thanks to:*

My parents, who raised me with a spiritual aware-
ness, although I did not necessarily agree with its
methods or teachings.

My second husband, who encouraged me to have
an open mind and explore an alternative spirituality
to find my true identity. Also for being the person
who made our move to Cornwall possible.

Those of the psychic community who encouraged
me to take part in workshops and the hosts of
development circles I attended.

Dear Arthur, as by visiting and conversing with
him, I was rewarded with a remarkable experience
from the spirit world.

My Reiki Master and Teacher, who taught me all
three levels of Reiki, introduced me to energies
that enhanced my spiritual development. To all
those I was privileged to provide treatments for,
and to the Reiki students I have taught.

My Reflexology tutor who sadly passed away. She
taught me well while trying hard to come to terms
with her own emotional issues.

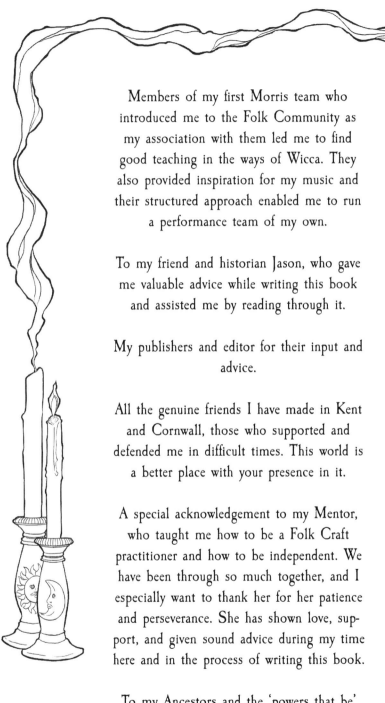

Members of my first Morris team who introduced me to the Folk Community as my association with them led me to find good teaching in the ways of Wicca. They also provided inspiration for my music and their structured approach enabled me to run a performance team of my own.

To my friend and historian Jason, who gave me valuable advice while writing this book and assisted me by reading through it.

My publishers and editor for their input and advice.

All the genuine friends I have made in Kent and Cornwall, those who supported and defended me in difficult times. This world is a better place with your presence in it.

A special acknowledgement to my Mentor, who taught me how to be a Folk Craft practitioner and how to be independent. We have been through so much together, and I especially want to thank her for her patience and perseverance. She has shown love, support, and given sound advice during my time here and in the process of writing this book.

To my Ancestors and the 'powers that be' for their ongoing guidance, support, and unconditional love.

# Author's Note

Hello dear reader...

I contemplated writing a book over ten years ago, when my Mentor released her own.

As my spiritual journey progressed over the years and I reflected back on the many things I had experienced, I realised what a fascinating story it would be to relate to others.

The book I produced was considerable in size. Therefore, my publishers suggested separating it into two publications. However, the main theme that runs through both of them is my connection with Cornwall and how it developed, hence the reason I included a brief overview of my childhood and family life.

My early spiritual development was also preparing me for my future in Cornwall. I knew that I was meant to be here for a reason, as the land constantly called me, but I did not understand exactly what that was.

My journey has been a 'roller-coaster,' and I thought it necessary to include the obstacles and challenges I faced as...oh boy...do the 'powers that be' test you on how much you really want this... particularly in Cornwall!

I have also included the rewards and wonderful things that have occurred, as they far outweigh any negative experiences.

This book is full of magic and mystical adventure. Please read on and let me take you on this extraordinary journey.

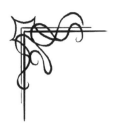

# Chapter 1
## Cornwall

*June 1967 – June 1978*

It was the first time my parents had driven three hundred miles for a vacation, and my father didn't have a plan. Our tiny three-wheeled car was bursting with luggage. I sat in the backseat with my brother and sister, surrounded by cream-coloured doors and a blue roof. My father drove, and my mother sat beside him, reluctantly accompanying him on this impulsive adventure. A bad reaction to tranquillisers had complicated her agoraphobia and emotional issues, so my father whisked us away to experience the healing energies of Cornwall after a woman from our church recommended it.

We travelled nonstop all night to avoid traffic. Concerned that my father would fall asleep at the wheel, I stayed awake and talked with him most of the way. We arrived in the small town of Fowey, Cornwall around six o'clock the next morning. I had succumbed to drowsiness during the final part of our journey, and awoke to the wonderful smell of seaweed and the haunting cry of seagulls at the entrance of Ready Money Cove.

My father made a few enquiries and found accommodation in a local guesthouse owned by Rosella, a lovely Spanish woman who owned dresses and hair combs worn by traditional dancers. My mother loved Spanish culture and glamorous women like Elizabeth Taylor and Rita Hayworth, so she and Rosella immediately connected.

Our rooms looked out over Fowey Harbour and Polruan's cottages. My mother said it looked like someone had picked the cottages up and scattered them "all higgledy-piggledy" on the rocks. She would often refer to the place as "pretty little Polruan."

As we explored the village, the small engine of our family car struggled to climb the steep Cornish hills, and my father and teenage brother had to push it up the undulating roads with the help of a few tourists and locals. We settled at Ready Money Cove, where my father took a running jump and launched himself into the water. He floated on his back in the sea with only his head and feet visible, looking

1

up at the sky, his bright orange swimming trunks and ginger hair glowing like a beacon. My sister and I played in the shallow water, climbed rocks, and searched the rockpools for shells.

We also visited the Kingdom Hall in Fowey, the gathering place of the local Jehovah's Witnesses; even on vacation, we had our religious obligations. It was there we met Enid and Elsie, two fraternal twins. After the meeting, they invited us to their home for tea and cake.

Enid favoured the colour green, while Elsie preferred red. Draped in scarves and cardigans in their respective hues, they both styled their brown hair in a neat bun. Enid was a cook, and she baked delicious cakes amid the red cupboards and yellow walls of their kitchen-diner. My father loved her lemon buns and Hevva cakes, though his stomach didn't agree after eating too many. These lively, tall, and talkative ladies were also enthusiastic card players. The following years brought games of partner whist and euchre, which we played in their lounge, surrounded by the twins' knickknacks. We found their Cornish accent warm, gentle and comforting.

Enid told such funny stories and recited Cornish rhymes. I still remember one of her riddles: "Long legs, crooked thighs, little head, and no eyes." She promised to reveal the answer on our return the following year if we hadn't solved it by then (The answer was fire tongs!). Unlike her sister, Elsie was a strict spinster whose belief in well-behaved children shattered after spending time with my sister and me.

At the end of each vacation, Enid and Elsie stood in the narrow lane leading out of the town, waving both their arms until our car was out of sight. We cried as we did not want to leave them or Cornwall.

Ready Money Cove was the first beach I frequented, but the sea spirits there seemed to have a wicked sense of humour. After being swept off a rock by a huge wave and stung by a wasp, I decided I preferred Whitehouse Beach.
My father tried to teach my sister how to swim in the children's pool at Whitehouse. While he talked with a nearby couple, my sister wriggled out of his arms, and I watched as he lost her beneath the water, but when he lifted her out, I was relieved to see that she was not hurt . He later tried to teach me and promised to hold me up, but I was not confident that he would. Needless to say, he was unsuccessful.

A diving board at Whitehouse beach protruded from the walkway over the rocks, and it was an ideal place to lie face down and gaze into the hypnotic clear water at high tide. At low tide, I climbed the rocks hunting for pebbles, pocketing mother of pearl, and meeting the tiny creatures that hid in some of the shells.

When I was thirteen, my maternal grandmother and uncle joined us on one of our trips to Cornwall. She was excited—it was her first real vacation—but she also worried about leaving her old tabby cat, Bambi, at the kennel. Bambi's purring made a musical sound, and my grandmother would often say that she was singing to us.

As soon as we arrived in Cornwall, my grandmother became quite the mischievous person. She loved the risqué cartoon postcards in the shops and read them, despite my father's scolding. She walked into a male lavatory by mistake and emerged laughing. And at night, the 73-year-old woman would recite naughty rhymes and dance the can-can for us, raising her feet higher than her head. My dad repeatedly told us to go to sleep, but we couldn't stop laughing.

Halfway through our vacation, she wanted to contact her daughters to hear how her cat was faring. We waited outside the telephone kiosk for my father to finish the call. After he left the kiosk, he spoke privately with my uncle, who immediately visited a nearby Cornish Inn to purchase a miniature bottle of brandy. We later discovered her cat had died, and decided not to tell her the bad news until she returned home to avoid spoiling her vacation. All she could talk about on the way home was reuniting with her cat.

Two weeks later, she suddenly passed away.

Once we were home again, my mother missed Cornwall, so she built a kind of shrine to it in our kitchen-diner. She attached a large postcard of Polperro Harbour to the wall and gave it the appearance of a small window by constructing a frame and windowsill with curtains. I often sat at our kitchen table, staring at it and imagining that I could see the harbour and hear the gulls. My mother also purchased a ship's wheel barometer and draped it in a black fishing net that reeked of tar, but I loved the aroma.

Over the years, she collected postcards, ornaments, stones, and shells, despite my father's complaints about the extra weight they added to our luggage. At home, she would adorn the wall and the surface of our dining room sideboard with her treasures. However, she would never bring home any ornamental piskies, saying they represented evil spirits, and warning us to not look at them when we passed them in the Cornish gift shops.

When I was fifteen, we returned to Cornwall, and stayed in a guest house in Mevagissey that overlooked the harbour. I sat by the window of my top-floor bedroom, gazing at an odd circular building near the sea wall. Later, while exploring the harbour alone, I met an artist. His illustrations inspired me, so I purchased a sketch pad and pencils, and returned to my room to draw the strange building from my window.

Behind that building and a mile across the sea, stood a large white house owned by an older woman who was being cared for by a registered nurse. I had no way of knowing at the time how much that nurse would later change my life.

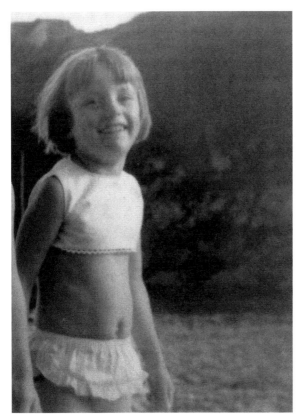

– 5 years of age on first vacation at Ready Money Cove.

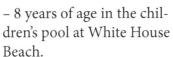

– 8 years of age in the children's pool at White House Beach.

16 years of age at Mevagissey harbour.

– Ready Money Cove looking out to sea

–The Fowey guest house we stayed in for our first vacation.

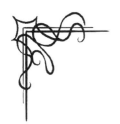

# Chapter 2

## Freedom

*June 1979 – April 1995*

My mother was vulnerable when the woman called at our home. One of my older brothers (who was only six at the time) was autistic, and committed to a residential home for the mentally impaired because of his violent rages. He was stronger than my mother at such a young age, and she was unable to care for him alone while my father was out at work. Separated from her child and devastated, my mother welcomed the woman, a Jehovah's Witness, who promised that my brother would be cured and live forever on a paradise earth.

This happened four years before I was born, and a short time after that visit, my parents converted. My early years and adolescence lacked birthdays and holidays, which were deemed too prideful and Pagan. Freedom of expression was prohibited, and the outside world was met with fear.

Despite this isolation, I went to school in Kent and excelled in music, drama, and English. I was given lead roles in school pantomimes, and was placed in higher achievement classes. My English tutor told my parents that I could qualify for enrollment at a London drama school, and I was offered a position at a school of higher education when I was about thirteen years old.

My parents worried that higher classes would lead to college, where they believed I would be tempted to indulge in drugs, alcohol, and wild parties. Instead, they encouraged me to leave school, find a part-time job, and engross myself in the Jehovah's Witnesses' preaching work for ninety hours each month, known as "pioneering."

I did not enjoy preaching, particularly during Christmas when some householders would become verbally aggressive towards my parents. I recall one such situation where a man shouted at my father, saying we should be opening presents at home, not knocking on strangers' doors on Christmas morning. I questioned some teachings, but didn't receive satisfactory answers. The elders noticed that I struggled against their control, and both they and my parents labelled me as troublesome and rebellious.

I reminded the elders of my mother's free spirit in the early days before she submitted to their rules. She appeared much younger than her age, and her shapely body and long, dark hair swayed to '60s music. Romani blood filled her veins, and she told me how her mother would bow and nod to the sun and moon. She loved Bohemian people, and had friends who lived in Romani caravans. Sadly, her free spirit eventually succumbed to her religion's dictates, and when this happened, she seemed to age quickly.

I met a man named Derek during a work experience placement, and we dated for about a year. I thought he resembled James Dean. My parents tried to stop me from seeing him by collecting me from my workplace, as the only time we could meet was when he accompanied me on my journey home.

One day, when the committee of elders wished to speak to me on another matter, I seized my chance and told them that I wanted to leave the sect. I knew that being disfellowshipped meant church members and my family would shun me. I didn't think it would make much difference, because I didn't feel wanted anyway, but nothing could prepare me for how this would affect me in the future.

The elders told my parents to cut off any emotions toward me. We spoke little, but when we did, it was about me leaving their home to live elsewhere. Their one requirement was that I get married, since they couldn't agree to me "living in sin" with Derek.

With nowhere else to go, I told Derek about my parents' mandate. Soon after, we married at the ages of seventeen and nineteen. I left home with everything I owned in a new suitcase and a few carrier bags. My mother accompanied me to the bus stop to help me with my bags. One of them contained soft toys, and a small teddy bear fell out. I saw sadness in her eyes as she carefully replaced it.

Derek and his mother, Joan, had lived in China with his father. After Joan's divorce, they moved back to the U.K. His father remained in China and only visited once a year, and the lack of contact distressed Derek. Joan felt guilty about her divorce and gave Derek the largest bedroom in her home, taking only a minimum payment from his wages for housekeeping. He had no curfew and didn't have to answer to her for anything.

Derek was an apprentice goldsmith with a jewellery company. He proudly showed me photographs of fabulous necklaces he created for royalty, celebrities, and the top retail outlets in Hatton Garden in London that sold his work. As the years passed, he also created many beautiful jewellery pieces for me.

On weekends, we frequented nightclubs. I had loved to dance from infancy, as it took me into another world and provided an 'escape' from reality. We explored Piccadilly Circus in the early hours of the morning along with my husband's friends, who played on fruit machines and occasionally disappeared for a while to view the x-rated movies. I was surprised to see so many people out and about in London so late at night.

Joan, heartbroken over her divorce, consumed alcohol frequently. She was Catholic and adored her three sons, but was disappointed she didn't have a daughter of her own, and welcomed me into her family. Life was different with them. Before I lived with Derek, I hadn't seen pornographic literature or movies, but he, his brothers, and his friends owned many magazines. Joan thought it healthy for young men to be interested in pornography, but I had difficulty understanding this and found it disturbing due to my religious upbringing.

Along with the new experiences came a new flavour of control. My marriage was a heady mixture of happy moments laced with domestic violence, emotional abuse, and insecurity. Derek was accustomed to defying rules and having his way. A crucifix hung on his bedroom wall, surrounded by large indentations. It was an altar to his anger. He had his caring moments, though. He put considerable effort into making my first Christmas celebration special. The weather even lent a helping hand by cloaking the landscape in snow. It felt magical.

After eighteen months of living with Joan, Derek and I moved into our own flat. Our relationship didn't improve, and I had an unexpected pregnancy. I didn't want to bring a child into our tumultuous relationship, but I also couldn't bring myself to terminate the pregnancy. My mother's warning that God would punish me for leaving her religion never left my mind. I often wondered if all of this turmoil was some form of divine retribution.

Yearning for support, I decided to return to the Jehovah's Witnesses. The elders heard my request and said I would have to attend all religious meetings at the Kingdom Hall for an undetermined amount of time to prove my commitment before reinstatement. During this time, the shunning continued. The elders often pressured women to dress in ways that wouldn't arouse them, and I was no exception. They criticised my clothing and makeup, and told me I would have to change them to meet their requirements. An elder even suggested I cut off my long hair, but my mother retorted, "So you want my daughter to look dowdy like your wife?" He denied this was his intention, and after six months, I was reinstated.

Derek didn't want to visit Cornwall due to its reputation for constant rain and little sunshine. His idea of a worthwhile vacation was to travel overseas, where he could find hot weather, topless female sun-worshipers, and a wild nightlife stocked with recreational drugs. I tried to persuade him to visit Cornwall, knowing that our two-year-old daughter Tammy would love it. Eventually, Derek agreed to try it.

It had been six long years since my last visit, so I looked forward to seeing Cornwall again. It constantly called to me, and I only felt complete when I was there. My parents helped by arranging accommodation in a static caravan owned by local religious acquaintances. It was wonderful to be there, but it rained most of the time during our stay, confirming for Derek that he was right to avoid the place. We sat in the caravan one afternoon, watching the torrential rain hit the windows. Derek furiously ranted, while I tried to distract Tammy with board games.

The wet weather didn't stop me from venturing out to see the stunning views and feel the energies of the land. I was determined not to let Derek's attitude spoil this vacation for Tammy and me. I knew it would probably be a long time before we returned.

We visited a childhood friend of mine, Louise, who lived in St. Stephens with her husband, and we reminisced. Louise informed me that Elsie, one of the twin sisters in Fowey, had passed away a few years ago. However, Louise had also left the religion, so she had no contact with church members.

I decided to visit Elsie's sister, Enid, to see how she was coping on her own, and I knew that she would love to meet Tammy. When we arrived at the twins' cottage, Enid's son answered the door and gave us the sad news that she, too, had recently passed away. He was there sorting out her belongings and invited us in.

I sat in the kitchen, solemnly looking around. Enid and Elsie's knickknacks were still where I remembered them, but covered in a thick layer of dust. There was a figurine of a woman wearing a blue ball gown, and another of a man wearing Regency attire on the mantelpiece in the lounge. As a child, I would carefully move them to music as though they were dancing together. I could almost smell the delicious food the twins made, and hear the Cornish rhymes they would recite while studying their playing cards. I also remembered the laughter that filled their home. How I loved and missed them.

As I sat there, Derek conversed with Enid's son. I overheard them discussing the plans for selling the property.

Three years later, my marital situation worsened considerably after Derek and I spent a disastrous vacation in Spain. My hope for a better relationship was dwindling, and no matter how hard I tried, it made no difference to him.

Two of my sisters-in-law spoke frankly to me about my marriage. One said that if I stayed with Derek, family and friends would no longer listen to my problems. She suggested I make plans to leave. The other reminded me that I was still young enough to begin a new life and another relationship. I knew they were right, but didn't act on their advice until a social worker told me that social services wouldn't allow Tammy to continue witnessing domestic violence. If I didn't leave, they would take her away.

On New Year's Eve 1988, Derek met a woman and began an affair with her without my knowledge. I also met a young man at a local naturist club named Paul. I frequented this club while working as a photographic model, as the grounds were ideal for assignments. Paul decided to do something completely different, as his friends usually arranged nights out while he was at work, and had no plans that evening. A colleague recommended visiting a naturist club, and Paul liked the thought of having an all-over tan in the summer. He discovered that they also had social evenings and decided to try one. My friend, Tifele, was attracted to him, so we invited him to a private party we were attending. He was a confident police officer, and I found him easy to talk with that evening. Unfortunately, he left the party early, because he had to work an early shift the next day.

When the new year began, I decided it was time to leave Derek, and we both began to lead more separate lives. I had evenings out with Tifele, and he went out with his friend. I met Paul again three months later when we attended the same club over Easter weekend. We were inseparable that weekend, and when I told him about my abusive marriage, he said it was time I found someone who could make me happy. Paul invited me to visit his one-bedroom cottage, where I felt comfortable and safe. He had lived alone for ten years, but wanted a family of his own, and it felt like fate had sent him to me during this difficult time.

Paul was concerned for mine and Tammy's safety, so after only two days of knowing him, I left Derek and moved into his home. I hoped that we would be safe with a policeman. The alternative was living alone, and with that, the strong possibility of volatile harassment from Derek.

I could talk with Paul for hours. He was mature beyond his twenty-six years, and I basked in his knowledge about life after being so restricted. He was my selfless and handsome knight in shining armour who promised to protect and care for my daughter and me. It was easy to fall in love with him.

Three weeks after my divorce was finalised, Paul and I married. We had lived together for nine months already and would have waited longer, but my parents were asking where I lived and would not have approved of us "living in sin."

Paul saw the huge amount of affection I gave Tammy, and at first, he thought it was unnatural. His mother had been raised in a children's home after her mother died while giving birth to her, and lived there until her father remarried, so he said he didn't experience physical maternal love. Paul and I helped each other heal the cycle of trauma: I gave him an abundance of affection, and in return, he helped me cope with the issues from my past.

We moved from his one-bedroom cottage to a three-bedroom house a few months after our marriage. Tammy was delighted to have her own room again after sleeping in the lounge on a folding bed without complaint. Our new home was only four years old—a small but beautiful terraced house with an open-plan interior. We lived in a cul-de-sac opposite a small green that led to a footpath and a local wood-land. Beyond the woodland, we discovered the ruins of an eleventh-century church. Despite living near a busy main road and a renowned car racing circuit, the area was surprisingly quiet and rural.

Paul had pleasant childhood memories of family vacations in Cornwall, and his paternal cousins lived in Somerset. His paternal family was warm, and they welcomed Tammy and me into the family with open arms. After two years of marriage, Paul and I discussed having another child. I thought it would strengthen the family bond, and it felt right to give him a child of his own. I wanted a son so that Tammy would be the only female child, which would lessen any feelings of rivalry. I researched scientific theories on conception and followed the advice given. I conceived three months later, and my first scan revealed that the foetus was male. Both of my childbirths were traumatic experiences that resulted in emergency caesarean sections. I refused blood transfusions, because I was worried about how my parents would react if they walked into my hospital room, and I didn't like the thought of someone else's blood in my veins. My decision caused additional complications, but thankfully, I survived on both occasions.

Life with Paul was secure and relaxed until repressed feelings began to surface. I attended regular counselling sessions and took a counselling course to help abuse survivors. I had to process my own trauma to help others, and it wasn't an easy task. Paul encouraged me to meditate, but I was reluctant, because my parents had taught me that silencing the mind made it vulnerable to demonic possession.

I had tried to meditate when I was younger. During my last family vacation in Cornwall, one of the young men I dated had practised transcendental meditation. His name was Ryan, and he was the son of the Spanish woman whose top floor apartment we rented during our first visit. He and I lay on the sand at Par Beach one warm sunny day, looking up at the sky as he explained the process. Even though I tried, I couldn't relax or give in to the process. I contacted Ryan again recently, and discovered he was in a meditation cult during those years. He developed mental health problems, and since then, has publicly campaigned against all religious cults. Paul knew little about my parents' religion, so he requested a bible study to understand my upbringing and the issues I faced. My parents assumed he would convert and were delighted, but his friends and family were concerned. Paul was known to do unusual things just to get a reaction from them. I explained to him some of the teachings and views I disagreed with, but was determined to let him decide for himself.

We attended religious meetings, and it wasn't long before the elders informed him that he couldn't continue to be a police officer if he intended to become a Jehovah's Witness. After hearing this, Paul cancelled his bible study and no longer attended their meetings. I still had questions and no satisfactory answers, so I wrote a letter to the body of elders, disassociating myself from the organisation.

After that, I started meditating. I purchased a pair of midnight blue candlesticks decorated with golden sun, moon, and stars. Like meditation, my mother had warned me that such items would invite demonic forces, but after I bought them, I waited and nothing happened. Nothing changed. Nothing, except me.

–Nightclubbing Days

–Second Marriage

– With Tammy

– With Ruben.

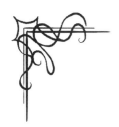

# Chapter 3
## Awakening

*July 1995*

During the summer of '95, Paul and I visited a marketplace in Kent that had a variety of stalls selling new and vintage items. One displayed hanging crystals that glistened in the sunlight and swayed in the breeze to beautiful music. As I listened and watched the crystals dance, something stirred within me. I asked the vendor about the music. It was from an album called Daintree Dreamtime by Ken Davis. I purchased it, and to this day, the music evokes fond memories of my initial awakening.

The New Age and occult scene had not fully emerged at this time, and I was unsure of where to find any information on witchcraft. I even searched the yellow pages under the letter "w" and found nothing. On reflection, searching through a telephone directory under Witchcraft is rather amusing.

May, Paul's mother, invited us to her yearly birthday barbecue in August. The venue was a small woodland near Eastbourne that she and her husband, Kevin, had purchased from friends of ours. A large gateway opened up to a row of tall trees. I heard the crunch of soft bark beneath our feet as we walked further from the entrance and into the woods. Tall trees huddled together near a small, flowing stream at the farthest boundary. I stood there, listening to the gurgling water and inhaling the aroma of wild garlic. This land was indeed a magical place.

When I met Suzie, the daughter of May's friends, she hugged me and brought the strong scent of patchouli with her. She was a sturdily built woman with short dark hair and spectacles, and wore the typical long crushed-velvet attire. We immediately noticed that we were both wearing pentacles. I had purchased mine from a local psychic fair in Kent, and not long after, I passed a young woman from my parent's church while shopping in a supermarket. She stared at me and her eyes

16

widened in terror when she saw the necklace.

Suzie was a witch, but this wasn't the first time I had met someone who identified as such. While visiting some friends, Derek and I met a married couple who claimed they were witches. Our friends were intrigued, but I immediately left with Derek, still influenced by my parent's religious warnings against witchcraft. A decade later, I was delighted to meet Suzie, and I had so many questions for her.

Our conversation was cut short, because May disapproved. She was a Christian, after all, and it was her birthday. She was also a tutor of nurses by trade—a high-ranking position in the medical community—who disliked some holistic services. To her, some of these methods deceived people and exploited them financially. She also disapproved of my past modelling work, and believed that women should use their brains to succeed in life rather than their bodies. I tried to explain that I had entered the profession to prove to myself that I was as desirable as the models Derek obsessed over, but it was far from who I truly was. Even so, May continued to be extremely judgmental, despite her own flaws and failures.

Soon after the barbeque, Suzie invited me to her home and promised to show me her altar. She lived only three miles away from me in a two-bedroom flat with her partner and their four children. As I entered her home, the aroma of incense enveloped me, and the haunting voice of a woman singing to the solitary beat of a drum wafted from her speakers.

I studied Suzie's magical tools, which were laid out on a small tiled hearth, while she explained their uses. Before visiting, I envisioned something more elaborate but was equally fascinated by their simplicity.
Suzie handed me a copy of Pagan Dawn magazine, which advertised local events, and included a contact page for group moots and coven advertisements. She described herself as a "hedge witch" and lent me two books: Hedge Witch by Rae Beth and Witchcraft – A Beginner's Guide by Teresa Moorey.

After our four-hour conversation, I left with arms full of literature. I immediately subscribed to the Pagan Dawn magazine, and purchased a large folder to begin a magical journal. I wrote out the Sabbat rituals from Teresa Moorey's book, and I occasionally still refer to them, combining some of her ideas with my own.

Suzie invited me to her local Pagan moot, where I met an attractive, mixed-race woman named Bella. She had also been a Jehovah's Witness, and like me, eventually chose Paganism. Bella connected me with a man known as Tom the Scottish Pagan, who lived in London and could provide me with more information about the Pagan scene.

After chatting on the phone with Tom, Paul and I travelled to London on his motorcycle. I rarely rode with him as a pillion passenger, but it was an easy way to travel through London, especially since Tom's residence was an apartment near the Thames river.

Tom was an amiable man who spoke with a broad Scottish accent. He was stockily built, of average height, and had long, strawberry-blonde hair. As Tom stirred our mugs of tea, he mentioned that he was vegan and only kept milk for guests. He also matter-of-factly shared his views of Paganism, but warned us that we would meet many "space cadets" during our spiritual journey. How right he was!

During our conversation, my eyes gravitated toward a large deep red velvet curtain that obscured one section of the room. Tom said it concealed the temple area for his Coven. Curious as I was, I didn't think it appropriate to ask for a viewing.

Tom suggested we attend some of the London events, particularly the Beltane and Halloween Gatherings at Conway Hall. He also advised us to continue attending the local moot, but most importantly, not to rush into anything, as the right path would eventually appear. Paul agreed, but I was hungry for knowledge and experience, so patience wasn't an option for me. Fortunately, Suzie had given me enough information to begin my studies.

It had been eleven long years since my last visit to Cornwall in 1985. Paul said that he would only agree to go if we visited a new area, rather than the familiar places from my childhood. He suggested North Cornwall: wild, rugged, natural, and non-commercialised. He was certain I would love it there. Unfortunately, we were victims of the negative equity trap in the early '90s and couldn't afford holiday accommodation, so we borrowed a caravan from generous friends.

Set on a clifftop, the Trevethy campsite in Tintagel greeted us with high winds. Paul and I struggled to set up our awning while our children, Tammy and Ruben, explored the site on their bicycles. This area resonated deeply with me, especially when standing on the cliffs and watching the ocean. I could easily have spent hours there watching, listening and feeling its energy.

We heard that a storyteller performed at the Camelot Castle Hotel in town, so we took the children to see her. One story featured the local Post Office, and explained that the building's roof was curved, because a dragon regularly sat on it.

Ruben adored dragons and loved that story. There were also darker, more disturbing tales told that night that remained in Ruben's memory throughout his life. They were not, in my opinion, the type of stories young impressionable minds ought to hear, but no warnings were given before the show.

With the small amount of money I possessed, I purchased an album entitled The Sorcerer by Phil Thornton from Merlin's Cave gift shop in Tintagel. There was a strange buzzing sound in the background I couldn't identify, and I later discovered that a bullroarer caused it. Years later, I understood why this music and sound of the bullroarer resonated profoundly with me and why it is ideal for energy raising. Tammy and I played the music in our car at the campsite, enjoying the heavy drum beat pulsing through the speakers, but Paul told us to keep the volume low so we wouldn't disturb the other tourists.

King Arthur's castle ruins are steeped in ancient history. Though there is some controversy around whether or not the castle belonged to King Arthur, it's a place that powerfully activates the imagination. Just before our visit, Paul purchased a toy sword for Ruben, who later put it to good use by chasing imaginary soldiers. Paul even helped him reenact the story of the "Sword in the Stone" by wedging the sword between two rocks.

We travelled along the narrow lanes to Boscastle until we were high up on a hill, where the coastline stretched out before us, catching glimpses of the valley below. The road guided us deeper into yet another mysterious and magical world. We explored the harbour, walking out to the cliffs and sitting on the rocks while listening to the sea and the gulls. There's a blowhole in the cliffs, and when the sea is at the right level, the waves rush into it before being pushed out again with a haunting roar that sounds like a dragon.

When we arrived at the Museum of Witchcraft in Boscastle, we were greeted unexpectedly by a clinical atmosphere and bright fluorescent lighting. A life-size mannequin of an attractive young woman lay on an altar with a strip of cloth draped between her separated legs while a chalice balanced on her pubic bone. A painting depicted a naked woman lying on the floor beside a hearth while a green horned spirit hovered over her. The illustrations brought to mind my parents' warning about occult practices and how they can invite demonic forces. There was another illustration of a man with a human torso and the legs and feet of a goat. His face, hair, and beard resembled Paul, and we all laughed.

The most potent presence within the room was a large goat god, which sat on a carved vintage throne. The goat's eyes were bright and alive, and as I looked deeply into them, I sensed it wished to impart knowledge of matters yet to be revealed.

It shocked me to read accounts of witch hunts and the hideous tortures women endured when accused of witchcraft. The victims were people who had unusual talents within the community, such as natural healing. Jealous rivals singled out others. Attractive women were also charged with bewitchment by men who desired them or wives who envied them. Of course, Christian dogmas justified all of the allegations and punishments. But how could Christianity claim that witchcraft is evil when it was the Christians who were abusing and torturing other human beings?

Gary, the museum owner, told me about an experience he had out on the moors on a dark moon phase. He said it was so dark that he couldn't even see his hand in front of his face. I asked him about local rituals and moots, but Gary was understandably protective of his knowledge and unwilling to share it with the thousands of tourists who visited the Museum. I yearned to live locally and become more involved with the Museum and its activities.

We returned to the Trevethy campsite the following year for another vacation. While exploring, Paul and I discovered a path leading down the cliffs into Rocky Valley. The presence of the faer folk was tangible, and we could feel their watchfulness as we journeyed through the woodland. Ruben darted here and there, hiding in bushes and jumping out to startle us. He instantly connected with the mischievous elemental spirits, and no matter how fast he ran through the woods, he didn't stumble over the uneven ground. Tammy was older now, and her long legs carried her up the rocks at incredible speed. One moment she was climbing, and the next, she was on top of the cliffs, waving at us.

We discovered the remains of a mill house in the valley. The walls were still standing, but the doors and windows were empty cavities. Inside the wall, there were two carvings of Cretan or Labyrinth mazes used in magical and meditative practices. The maze's path is traced from the outside towards the centre using one's index finger, and this action induces an altered state of consciousness. With practice, it can even transport the practitioner into the Otherworld.

I photographed Ruben playing in the mill house, and while studying the image, I noticed a bright light above his shoulder. A winged figure gleamed inside the light—could it have been the faer folk?

Ribbons and other objects known as "clouties" were tied to the trees. Offerings of fruit and food rested on a slate ledge above the mazes, and small crystals, stones, and coins protruded from gaps within the rock face. As we left the mill house and crossed a bridge over a flowing stream, I noticed a young woman on the other side by a tree. She gently pulled out a strand of her long dark hair and entwined it around the overhanging branch as she prayed. It was an emotional experience as I could feel the strength of the energies surrounding me, drawing me over the threshold into the Otherworld.

The river widened further along the valley, and a stiff breeze moved through the trees. I hadn't experienced air so pure since I received oxygen before my emergency caesarean section when I gave birth to Ruben. Paul informed us we were nearing St. Nectan's waterfall, and even though we had walked for a long time, the thought of seeing it energised me. The lush green trees in the glen gracefully welcomed us as we passed, and I paused on a wooden bridge to listen to the deep, babbling stream that mimicked human voices. Blood-red oxide coated the larger stones within the stream. According to legend, this is the blood of King Arthur's wounded soldiers, which poured out as they staggered to the ancient hermitage near the waterfall.

We ascended a path leading to the top of the waterfall and entered a small gateway to a paved patio area with white garden chairs and tables. The owners, Ben and Jill, welcomed us and offered tea and refreshments. Photographic evidence of spirits and orbs captured by tourists hung on a corkboard. While we rested, I read a pamphlet about the site's history, and discovered that a building, now known as the Hermitage, once stood near the waterfall and belonged to St. Nectan in the sixth century. Legend has it that St. Nectan rang a silver bell to warn ships about the rocks during storms. Though the bell is no longer there, some claim to have heard its haunting tones late at night.

After tea, we descended the steep slate steps to the bottom of the waterfall. Legend says that the waterfall may have been used for ceremonial purposes. Initiates would jump from the top ledge and ride the strong, flowing water through a large bowl-shaped cavity within the rock which resembles a female pelvis, as part of a symbolic ritual for rebirth. The top ledge wasn't accessible at this time due to health and safety restrictions, so we continued our descent to the bottom.

The waterfall appeared from behind a protruding rock in all its splendour. It reached about twenty feet high, and the water cascaded down with tremendous force. Visitors were blessing themselves with the water, and there were more clouties on the trees and offerings on the rocks nearby. I could not understand why some visitors felt a need to carve their names and symbols on the rock face, as this damaged and spoiled its natural beauty.

When I entered the meditation room at the top of the waterfall, I saw statues of gods and goddesses. A small fountain trickled water into a granite wall. Tea light candles were provided for visitors, but the box of matches left to light them had become damp in the moist air. A book lay beside them for visitors to record their experiences. Many left photographs of deceased loved ones with notes asking the gods to watch over them, and children left relics from deceased pets.

I had packed a long black robe with the hopes of taking a dramatic photo. The robe was part of a project that I created for a cosmetic competition while taking a Beauty Therapy course in college. My entry was entitled "Moon Goddess." I dressed my model in the robe, along with a silver turban adorned with a glittering crescent moon, and applied silver and pale blue cosmetics to her face. I had won first place in a previous cosmetic competition, and represented my college in the Brighton International Make-Up Competition. Because of these achievements, I received the Student of the Year Award in 1997.

When my course began, I developed a deeper connection with the moon. At the end of each day, I walked through the college car park, exhausted from my intense coursework, and looked up at the moon shining down on me with motherly energy. It was as if she were saying, "I am here." I was aware of her presence with me on my journey home most evenings and referred to her as "Mother Moon." The Jehovah's Witnesses didn't permit the use of idols or symbols to connect with God, and I found it difficult to communicate with something I couldn't see. The moon gave me the comfort I wasn't receiving from my own mother, and provided the focal point I needed to connect with the divine.

Toward the end of our vacation in Cornwall, Paul and I walked to the cliff edge at Trevethy, where I donned the black robe and all its meaning and asked him to take a photograph. Strong winds almost knocked me off balance, but I was happy with how the photo turned out, and it continues to remind me of my initial awakening.

– Camelot Castle Hotel Tintagel

– King Arthurs
Castle Tintagel

– First Visit to
the Museum
of Witchcraft

– St Nectans
Waterfall

– The 'Awakening'
photo of me on
the cliffs

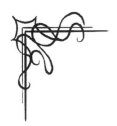

# Chapter 4
## First Steps

*August 1997*

Our visit to Cornwall in 1997 inspired me to change my home decor. I had in the past accepted Paul's ideas on decorating and furnishing a home, which he learnt from his mother, who had a preference for Laura Ashley design. I found it all rather straight-laced.

My mother, on the other hand, was completely different. She loved to experiment with colours and painted each wall of our kitchen-diner a different colour of orange, pink, and green. She loved the psychedelic era and was a woman with a wild and free Romani spirit until her religion eventually robbed her of that side of her personality.

I had inherited my mother's wild and free spirit, so on our return home from Cornwall, Paul and I visited a store to purchase deep purple paint and a circular bath sponge. We removed the Laura Ashley wallpaper and the floral dado border that separated the lower papered section of beige and gold stripes from the pale pink paint on the upper half. Our home was an open-plan abode, so I began to apply the purple paint with the sponge over the pale pink walls, covering the walls of the dining room, lounge, stairwell, and upper floor that led to the bedrooms.

My father-in-law, Kevin, visited while I was in the process of doing this. I brewed him a mug of tea, and he sat on a chair, arms folded, watching me sponge-paint the walls. The only word Kevin uttered frequently was "Blimey!"

I purchased new furniture, including two cream two-seater couches, and hung pictures of zodiac signs, a moon goddess, and an illustration a young student from college had drawn for me of a god and goddess figure. There was also an enlarged photo of me standing on the Cornish cliffs that Paul had taken. We fixed black iron candle holders to the wall as I frequently lit candles and burnt incense.

In the evenings, Paul and I sat on the couch with a glass of wine to relax and studied the purple walls. The sponge painting had created intriguing swirls forming many faces. Paul described the faces as tortured souls, but I did not see them in that way.

Paul's friends occasionally visited, and it was obvious they did not agree with the change in decor. One couple constantly redecorated their home in a similar conservative style. They did not express their feelings directly to us, but Paul's sister, who was a kitchen designer, hinted at their concerns when she visited Paul.

His youngest sister had a university degree and went on to have a career with a renowned world famous news and media organisation. She seemed to rate herself above her siblings. Paul was resentful he never received the attention from his parents that she did, as he thought he could have accomplished more if he had their support.

The first ritual I celebrated was on a full moon phase before the summer solstice of 1997. I had researched and studied for eighteen months and set up a sacred space in my lounge, ignoring any lingering doubts and fears from my religious upbringing. It took a huge amount of courage to take this step. My first altar was small, simple, and in the meantime, featured a pewter faerie that represented a goddess until Paul sculpted a statuette for me out of clay. I possessed the minimum of magical tools, but this didn't affect the energy raised. While Paul, Tammy, and Ruben were in their beds, I invoked spirits for the first time. I felt a breeze blow past me even though I was in my lounge, and a peaceful, gentle energy calmed my initial anxiety.

My first Sabbat ritual was a Summer Solstice celebration at noon on a hot summer day a few weeks later. I set up a ritual space in our garden using an ornate stone bench that doubled as the ideal altar. Irregular paving stones covered the ground. Nearby, a low stone border surrounded a small willow tree and a few small rose bushes. Our nosey neighbours watched us, and we gave them plenty to talk about. We weren't the only ones putting on a show, though. One neighbour often sunbathed topless in her back garden. Ruben, amused by this, even wrote a humorous song about it.

The closest sacred site to my residence was the Coldrum Long Barrow near Trosley Country Park. It is an ancient burial mound built and used over one thousand years before Stonehenge. The stones are no longer in their original position, so the people who study ancient sites cannot agree on what used to be there. In the late nineteenth century, Benjamin Harrison believed it was a stone circle like Stonehenge, but smaller. Despite disagreements between many scholars, it was finally decided it was a rectangular long barrow.

It is an ideal place to observe the sunrise on the Summer Solstice. Each year, I would set my alarm clock for half-past three that morning and drive to a small car park near the site. I walked through a small, wooded lane and across a beautiful poppy field in full bloom, admiring the vibrant scarlet heads that welcomed the summer season. I climbed the stile and walked along a narrow pathway that sloped upwards to the top of the barrow. A few friendly Pagans gathered there, and we enjoyed the sunrise together.

After a year of celebrating sabbats and moon phases—and even more study and research—I felt ready to perform a self-initiation ritual to the gods that I found in Hedge Witch by Rae Beth. My preparations began near Beltane in 1998, an auspicious time of year for initiations and new beginnings. I bathed in saltwater, used specific oils, and followed each step carefully. The initiation between myself and the ancestral spirits alone was one of the most important steps I've taken during my spiritual journey.

I updated my magical journal regularly with rituals, meditations, dreams, and discoveries. It's been a helpful reference and a reminder of how much I have accomplished. The first spell I cast was to ask the gods to help me find a wisewoman who would guide my development. It took many years to come to fruition, and taught me that requests to spirits don't always bring immediate results. I now understand the phrase, "when the student is ready, the teacher will appear." Spells often manifest in the way you least expect, so be careful what you wish for!

Friends of mine had often mentioned Alice, a local spirit medium they had visited for consultations, and marvelled at her accuracy. I knew two young men who had a spiritual reading with her the evening that Kieron, a mutual friend, tragically passed away in a car accident in 1985. Alice wrote down the information she received from Spirit and gave it to them. They later read it to me, and it accurately described Kieron's injuries and the circumstances surrounding his death. He was only twenty-six years old, and his daughter was born six weeks after he died.

Twelve years passed before I decided to book an appointment with Alice. Her home stood on a busy road next to an old, abandoned garage filled with rusted, abandoned cars. I noticed a faded yellow wooden crescent moon swaying in the breeze just above her door as I walked toward it. Alice's daughter invited me in and guided me to the lounge. I sat on an armchair and admired a collection of large crystal balls in a glass display cabinet. The spiritual presences in the house were palpable.

Alice was a short woman with bright bleach-blonde hair and a rugged complexion. She welcomed me into her dining room, which smelt of cigarettes, and gestured towards a chair behind a polished oval mahogany table. Beside her lay a deck of old, worn Tarot cards. Before arriving, I had removed all of my jewellery, so there were no external clues that might invalidate the experience. I also brought a cassette tape to record the reading, and Alice wrote down messages as she received them.

She spoke of my paternal grandmother, who passed away during my infancy. I knew little about her, but Alice said she was the spirit who walked with me and held my hand. She also mentioned a name that belonged to my piano teacher, but Alice insisted it was my grandmother's name. Later, when Ruben was building his family tree for a school project, Paul contacted my parents to confirm his grandparents' names. We discovered that Alice was correct, and the name she gave also belonged to my grandmother.

Alice also told me I had been executed for healing others successfully in a past life during the 17th century. She revealed my former name and said I was one of four sisters who died at the age of twenty-two, and was subsequently buried in Cornwall near the Tamar. I felt as though half of me remained in Cornwall when I returned to Kent and wondered if this was the reason. I consulted with a historian, and discovered that no one as young as 22 was ever executed in Cornwall. She identified my connection with Cornwall, but she may not have a strong connection to past lives. She was accurate about things she couldn't have known, so she didn't use "cold reading," where a person reads the client's body language and facial expressions. This proved to me her connection with the spirit world was her strength.

Alice shared a message from my relatives in the spirit world. They were proud of me for having the courage to break free from my parents' religion and follow my own path. After so much struggle and loss, this was confirmation that I'd done the right thing.

After coming home from work one evening, Paul described a domestic disturbance he dealt with in London. The resident was an alleged vampire, and his colleagues didn't want to investigate, so Paul volunteered out of curiosity.

When he arrived at the apartment, he met a witch named Sophia, who suffered from chronic fatigue syndrome, and shared the space with a younger man named Jay. The vampire no longer lived there, but still had a powerful influence over Jay. She had practised her craft for twenty-seven years and wanted to start a teaching coven. Paul showed her a photograph of me that he kept in his wallet and she gasped, commenting on the power of my eyes. He suggested we visit her so that I could meet her, and it was the first time I met someone associated with vampires.

Sophia lived in an apartment inside a beautiful Victorian property near Crystal Palace Park, and greeted us at the door in a short black dress with a crimson kiss. She was middle-aged, willowy, and pale, with cropped dark hair. As we entered her lounge, I immediately noticed a large picture of an Egyptian pharaoh leaning against the wall. A huge athame lay alongside other magical items on a highly polished sideboard on the opposite side of the room. Sophia told us how the vampire emotionally abused her, yet she was still in love with him. She knew he drained her psychically and believed that this was the cause of her illness, and although she tried to cast protection spells to keep him away, she continued to feel drained by him.

Jay was 22 years old, and his dark eyes appeared almost black as he intently stared at us. His Gothic attire and make-up emulated the main character from the movie The Crow, which he spoke about passionately. Sophia tried to help Jay with his problems, but felt drained by him due to his connection with the vampire. The negative energy there was evident, and although Sophia wanted her life to improve, she found it difficult to break free. On a separate occasion, I heard the vampire appeared at a protest in a park a few years ago, where activists had tied themselves to a tree to prevent it from being cut down. He dressed in costume and visited them at night while wielding a knife.

I offered to cast protection spells for Sophia and provide healing treatments. Paul also gave her financial advice, but unfortunately, she didn't heed it. I saw a certificate from the High Church of Magical Arts on her wall, and I found it hard to understand why she couldn't extract herself from this situation, considering her magical qualification. Perhaps the way of the vampire had become part of Sophia, and she required energy from others to replenish what the men in her life were draining.

After a while, Paul and I stopped visiting Sophia since she made no effort to help herself. This experience taught me that when Pagans claim high ranking statuses and hold magical certificates, their qualifications remain useless unless they have inner strength and discipline.

Suzie, the hedgewitch, invited me to a Wiccaning ceremony for her youngest child. I had attended some of her group rituals, and although I enjoyed them, I felt a little uncomfortable about the presence of small children. The ceremonies often took place in local public woodland where passersby would hear chanting and the cries of infants. They would hover around the space, peering through the trees to observe our activities. I could understand why they'd be concerned, especially with the media sensationalising connections between witchcraft and child sacrifice. I withdrew from attending local rituals because of this.

I first saw Kenneth, a male witch, on a TV program featuring stories on life's "strange and absurd" aspects. I noted his details and called him on the phone. Kenneth referred to himself as the "King of Witches." Our conversation revolved mainly around him and his achievements, such as his 600-member coven, and he dodged any direct questions I asked. I didn't contact him again, and discovered years later that he earned a dubious reputation within the Pagan scene.

Paul wasn't doing well financially at this time, so while visiting a local marketplace, I sought advice from a crystal seller. She advised me to keep a small citrine crystal in my purse to ensure it would never be empty. I bought two crystals and gave one to Paul. I hoped it would help his financial situation, and I also wanted to make sure we were able to visit Cornwall for the total eclipse of 1999, as it was the only area of the United Kingdom where it would be visible in its entirety. An experience such as this would be too rare to miss.

This event could attract thousands of tourists to sacred sites, resulting in severe land damage. To protect these landmarks, a group known as Pagans in Cornwall performed magical work to awaken elemental guardians known as "Spriggans." I joined them in this work at home and created a personal chant for energy raising:

*"I conjure power to send to the West*
*Wake up ye Spriggans from thy rest*

*Hear the words that come forth from my lips*
*And protect the Cornish land at the time of eclipse.*
*Spriggans heed the words I say*
*And protect the sacred sites that day*
*From all the people who could inflict harm*
*Upsetting the balance and causing alarm.*
*We will assist to protect these sites*
*By conducting rituals, spells and rites.*
*We will set an example of the way*
*To treat these sites upon this day.*
*We will protect every site, tree and bough*
*Wake up ye Spriggans - prepare for it now!"*

I used the chant regularly during my rituals to help protect the land I loved. I researched Cornish phrases to include in my rituals for a deeper connection. The phrases are:

Behold the waters of life - (wer) An dowr a vywnans ma
This cup - (war) An hanaf ma
This well - (war) An puth ma
This sacred place - (war) An neves ma
May the Goddess and Ancestors bless - Bens bannath an dywow ha'gan hendasow war
Gods be with you - An dywow genowgh
And also with you - Ha gened-si ynwedh
Thank you- Meur ras dhis.
So be it - Beddens yndellma
Let the gates be opened - Bens an porthow igerys
Let the gates be closed - Bens an portow deges
Protection of the Gods on this place - Gwithyans an dywow war an le ma
May the Gods be honoured - Bens gordhyans dhe'n dywow
Sacred Fire - Tan Sakrys
We are here to honour the Gods - Ni'yw omma dhe ri gord dhe'n dywow.

I experienced powerful energy when I worked alone in this way, and was curious to see how much stronger the energy could be within a group. I discovered an advertisement in Pagan Dawn magazine requesting new members for an Egyptian group called The Temple of Selket, based only ten miles away from my home. I contacted Penelope, the priestess, and arranged for Paul and me to visit her.

Penelope lived in a large bungalow. Paul until then had assumed the homes of all Pagans were generally dirty, and he was impressed by Penelope's cleanliness. Penelope was an intriguing woman, small and thin, with wild, frizzy ginger hair. Her Egyptian artefacts fascinated me, particularly a hefty golden asp that stood by the entrance as a guardian. She believed that she was an Egyptian servant girl in a past life who was murdered by a dagger plunged into her back.

We had a long conversation about my life and magical experience. When she heard that my birth sign is Leo, she gestured towards a small golden statue placed in a prominent position on her shelf, saying I had something in common with this figure. It depicted Sekhmet, a sun goddess, who has the head of a lioness. I felt an instant connection with the figure, and it was hard to stop staring at it, as well as pay any attention to what Penelope was saying. Suddenly, Penelope decided to move from her position on the floor, as she sensed a strong energy passing between Sekhmet and me, and couldn't remain there for fear of levitating!

Penelope's group had five members, and she warned the magic they practised invoked powerful energies contrary to those of Wicca. She advised us how to 'ground ourselves' by visualising the roots of a tree growing from the soles of our feet deep into the earth. We would need to do this frequently during our rituals there. We got on well with her, and eventually joined her group. She had studied with the Fellowship of Isis, and advised us not to read books on Egyptian rituals, as her way of working would differ and interfere with our training.

Two days after meeting Penelope, Paul and I visited the same marketplace in Maidstone, where I was drawn to the stall with hanging crystals. I passed a stall that sold vintage clothing and noticed a cardboard box. It was overflowing with coloured fabric, but my eyes fell on a long, thin shape sticking out of the cloth. I reached in and pulled out an eighteen-inch wooden statue of Sekhmet. There were no other Egyptian artefacts on the stall, and I immediately purchased it.

The next time I visited Penelope, I took the statue along and told her how I found it. She replied that I was meant to find it, and after examining it thoroughly, determined it had experienced trauma, given its battered and dusty appearance. She said the statue needed to be calmed, because its energies were "rocking the room" and giving her a headache. Penelope covered the statue with anointing oils and held a hooked wand towards it for a few minutes. She also performed a ritual to "open the statue's mouth" at Sekhmet's request, which meant I would be required to provide regular food offerings. The statue also needed re-painting. Penelope suggested I visit the British Museum in London and study the Sekhmet statues for inspiration. I followed her advice, and when I returned home, I painted the statue black to resemble the ones I saw at the museum. It has been present throughout most of my journey as a protector and healer.

Paul and I joined his mother for a barbecue at her woodland, as he was helping his parents cut back some of the tree branches. I took my statue of Sekhmet with me, as I was forming a closer connection with it. I stood her on the table beside me while we were eating lunch, and placed a piece of bread at her feet.

May picked up the statue and asked "Is this your God?" I replied that I had recently acquired her and was researching information on the deity. May asked what it was made of, and then turned Sekhmet upside down and hit the statue's head against the edge of the table several times. This alarmed me greatly, as I knew Sekhmet would not tolerate disrespect. I sensed May's action was telling me that she did not believe in the deity, nor was she afraid of it.

There was one ritual we performed within the Temple of Selket that I will never forget. The lounge in Penelope's bungalow was at the end of a narrow corridor, which she said resembled the entrance of an Egyptian tomb. The group walked in procession along the corridor in funereal silence. I carried a bowl of burning charcoal and incense while Louise, another member, walked beside me, holding a candle. When setting up the sacred space and casting a circle, we visualised red light instead of the blue used in Wiccan ceremonies. We used Egyptian phrases for "Blessed Be" when invoking the elementals, and visualised four gigantic spitting snakes in the quarterly directions.

Penelope warned that we may feel their tongues strike our legs or feet as they approached. As Paul began to read an invocation for the God Set, the door at the bungalow entrance began to shake wildly. We were all startled, but Penelope urged him to continue reading, and the door shook until the invocation was complete. Penelope thought it may have been a confused spirit who suffered an unexpected death, but I felt it was Set showing his power.

An entry in my magical journal at this time has a description of one of my first meditations. A woman with short, spikey grey hair and a purple robe approached me. As we conversed, the word "Zana" entered my mind. I didn't know what it meant at the time, but I wrote it down anyway. The full meaning of this would not be revealed for another ten years. I hoped that maybe this woman symbolised someone I would meet in Cornwall.

– New home décor and my first shrine to the Gods.

– My first Altar.

– First garden ritual altar for Summer Solstice

– A garden night-time Full Moon ritual

– My Sekhmet

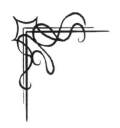
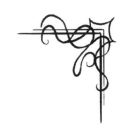

# Chapter 5

## Eclipse

*August 1999*

Paul had bought a four-berth caravan that needed renovation, and worked on it throughout the winter. We used it for the first time on our vacation to witness the solar eclipse in Cornwall in 1999. We had not travelled far, when our car overheated while towing the caravan, as the engine was too small to cope with the weight. Disappointed but determined, we returned home and Paul contacted his parents. They kindly offered to pay for a larger hire car so we would not miss our vacation. I was extremely grateful for this, as I had been so excited about this vacation. It would be the first time I had experienced a total eclipse.

We eventually arrived at Bossiney Camping and Caravan Park, about half a mile from Tintagel. Two other families were there who camped next to us and were excited about the eclipse. They told us about their plan to see a reenactment of the Battle of Camlann. We had never experienced a reenactment, so we decided to join them.

As we entered the field adjacent to the local church, we saw colourful tents and stalls selling items crafted by authentic methods used in mediaeval times. Men wore suits of armour or archery attire, and women wore mediaeval dresses and hats. Peasant's attire was made of linen and rough wool—materials considered cheaper in those days and not as comfortable—while the higher class wore smoother fabrics accented with beautiful embroidery and a stylish cut to the cloth. These were the costumes I admired most.

The reenactors waged two battles that day, along with some archery displays. The battles were like pantomimes: Arthur and Mordred's soldiers stood in opposition before charging toward one another. Their combat training made it look realistic, and the audience cheered with enthusiasm. Ruben enjoyed it, but Tammy was more interested in the clothes and jewellery stalls. While browsing the stalls, we met a lovely Welsh couple, Peter and Tania, who sold mediaeval garments, armour, and occult merchandise.

Peter created wonderful chalices, selenite crystal wands, and beautifully carved wooden platters, while Tania had dressmaking skills and created mediaeval and Pagan attire. Their items were more expensive than those on other stalls, but were also of excellent quality.

Paul and I arranged to meet Peter and Tania after the event in the bar of the Camelot Castle Hotel. It is similar to the Headland Hotel in Newquay, featured in The Witches movie. We relaxed in the lounge bar beside an expansive window, enjoying the fabulous view of the sea and watched the waves crashing against the cliffs. My heart ached to be there. I expressed my deep love of Cornwall to Peter and Tania, as well as our plan to move there in 2010 when Paul retired. They were considering doing the same, but their sons, who were a little older than Ruben, needed to finish their education before they could do so. We also discussed the eclipse and agreed to watch it together.

When we awoke that morning, Tintagel was buzzing with excitement. We met with Peter and Tania, and after some discussion, decided the best place to observe it would be on the cliffs next to King Arthur's castle. Weather reports had predicted the eclipse would occur at 11:11 that morning. We visited a retail outlet to purchase the eclipse viewers so that we could observe the sun without damaging our eyes. It was a dry, cloudy day, but fortunately, the cloud cover broke for a while, allowing us to see the moon's shadow as it slowly passed over the sun. We laid on the uneven ground, as it was easier than straining our necks to look upwards for a long period of time.

As I watched the creeping shadow in awe, I squealed with delight and spoke to the sun and moon, complimenting them on their combined beauty. The moment just before the total eclipse, thick clouds disappointingly covered the sun, so we stood up to observe the effects. A black shadow slowly crept over the sea and sky, and we heard a rumbling sound. Tammy was worried, as she believed media speculation about the eclipse marking the "end of the world," but Ruben jumped like a happy spring lamb. The temperature dropped, the wind whirled around us, and darkness shrouded us as seagulls and other birds cried out in confusion. In the distance, camera flashes glinted along the coastline amid the echoes of cheers and applause from miles away. The light gradually returned, and the clouds disappointingly obscured our view of the diamond ring effect that I would have loved to witness. A fellow therapist I knew had her vacation in Newquay to see the eclipse. The break in the clouds that we had, reached Newquay just in time for observers to see the total eclipse and 'diamond ring' effect. I was so jealous!

As I observed the eclipse from the north of Cornwall, way down west in deepest darkest Cornwall, someone I was yet to meet, watched it from a powerful stone circle...

When the eclipse was over, we slowly walked back to the campsite. The atmosphere and people around us were unusually quiet. There was a substantial energy shift, and I sensed nothing would be the same again after this experience.

At this time I developed a close friendship with Lisa, my Reflexology teacher. As well as teaching me, we were both studying an Aromatherapy course together at college. Lisa had suffered from depression since the age of eleven, as she had an unhappy childhood. I took her to nightclubs to cheer her up and bring some fun into her life. She had agreed to accompany us on our vacation to Cornwall to see the eclipse, but unfortunately changed her mind when she had a bout of depression. I wrote many letters to her during this vacation, updating her on all the places we visited, and she regretted not joining us. Lisa told me she stood outside in her garden smoking a cigarette as she watched the partial eclipse, and thought about us in Cornwall.

Back at the campsite we spent the evening with the other two families. One couple had a daughter a little older than Tammy, so they visited Tintagel that evening and met up with a group of boys. It was good for her to mix with other people her age while we were away, as the relationship with her boyfriend had become too intense. He wrote letters sending them to the campsite with passport photographs enclosed of himself looking miserable without her. He also phoned the nearby telephone kiosk to speak to her, so I was pleased that she socialised. One of the families set up a barbecue, and we shared food and drink together as they spoke of their plans to move to Cornwall. As the years passed, we occasionally met them and although they still spoke about it, it had not happened. Fantasising about a new life elsewhere and having the courage or opportunity to actually do so in reality are completely different. I was reluctant to leave Cornwall after this amazing experience, and felt down for a while after our return home.

–The Cliff beside King Arthur's Castle (where we viewed the eclipse)

– Watching the effects of the Total Eclipse

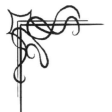

# Chapter 6
## Magical Influences

*August 1999 – August 2000*

I visited Penelope to tell her about the eclipse, and she shared some insights with me. During a meditation session with Sekhmet, the goddess revealed that Paul was draining me and preventing me from channelling energy. Penelope noticed he often took over when I tried to do anything myself. I had noticed this, but accepted it as his way of trying to help.

I asked Penelope if an active sexual relationship could drain one's energy and affect magical work. She replied that sex is the lowest form of energy, because of its connection with survival and its origination from the base energy centre of the body. A person requires less sexual activity as their development reaches a higher spiritual level. As the senses develop, one can attain a state of ecstasy from another person merely touching the energy field around their body, making physical interaction unnecessary.

Penelope was also concerned the energies weren't flowing well among us. She and another group member suspected that married couples working together were the source of the problem. She considered Paul a persuasive person who could talk people into believing anything he wanted them to, and advised me to raise protective barriers daily to prevent Paul from draining my energy. I knew that his occupational studies included psychology, which could have enhanced his ability to influence others.

Not all of Penelope's opinions and advice sat well with me at the time, though I realised years later that she was correct. She invited me to attend a new women's mystery group, but Paul didn't want me to go. He sensed that Penelope disliked him, and assumed there was a sexual relationship between her and another middle-aged single woman in the group. I didn't want to attend without him, so I declined the invitation.

Life was busy for me in 1999. Paul had been a supportive husband. He encouraged me with my ambitions for a career, as he wanted me to develop into a confident and competent person. I also pursued other interests throughout our marriage, and would not have achieved my qualifications without his support. Paul wanted me to experience all the things I should have at a younger age when my life was restricted. He promised me that no matter what I did, he would always be there for me.

I earned my diploma in beauty therapy at college and went on to study aromatherapy and reflexology. The clients I practised on would speak to me about their problems during beauty treatments, so I thought it more important to treat the 'inner person' rather than their appearance. I discovered that reflexology was thought to have Egyptian connections due to ancient images depicting one person holding the other's feet, possibly to massage them.

I also earned my first-degree Reiki qualification after travelling eighty miles to Saffron Walden in Essex for the course. I was fortunate to find an excellent Reiki teacher who had travelled to Japan to study the traditional method of Reiki, as the methods had changed considerably here. In the West, it is considered a complementary therapy rather than a practice for self spiritual development and healing. He taught the Japanese traditional way, but also included some Western practices, too.

Paul and I attended a local folk festival in Kent earlier that year. There were dancers, musicians, and a funfair on the castle grounds. I saw a group of Morris dancers who wore only black. The men had top hats, tattered shirts, and soot-coloured faces. The women had white painted faces, lips of ebony, and wore black velvet dress-coats that laced up the front with pointed handkerchief hemlines. They were Border Morris dancers with big sticks, sunglasses, and attitude. They differ from Cotswold Morris teams who dance with handkerchiefs and wear white.

As I watched them dance, I studied a woman who had the presence of a leader. I saw a pentagram on a silver chain around her neck and sensed she could have a similar spiritual path to myself. I considered approaching them, but their serious and unsmiling persona made them seem unapproachable. The heavy, rhythmic drum beats that fueled their dancing lingered with me for days after.

During the first week of October 1999, Paul, Ruben, and I attended our first Halloween Pagan event at Conway Hall in London, where renowned speakers lectured on various paths within witchcraft. We entered the main hall, where rows of chairs awaited audience members, and stalls stood at either side of the room. We sat in the front row and listened to Chris Gosselin, a slender man who wore a robe and wrote humorous songs about life as a Pagan. Many of them were quite risqué!

Ruben was a different and otherworldly little man. He was seven years old at the time, and laughed loudly at Chris's songs, even though he couldn't understand the meaning of the lyrics, so we left and explored the stalls in other rooms until Chris' performance ended. Ruben remained an avid admirer of Chris, but it wasn't until his teenage years that he understood the lyrics to his songs. I will never forget the sound of his raucous laughter and the tears that rolled down his face as he recited them.

Leonard, a member of our Egyptian group, also attended the Halloween event. He was a tall American man with a striking facial bone structure who resembled the actor Peter Cushing. He had a deep, charming voice and was also a member of the London Vampire Group.

We returned to the main hall to watch a performance that featured a Morris team. I was delighted to discover they were the same Gothic team I saw at the local folk festival in May. I was close enough to hear the lead female dancer firmly instructing one of the younger dancers during the performance, and saw immediately how disciplined they were.

During the break, two of the men in the group announced they were after "new blood" to join their team, and their banter made them seem less intimidating. We approached them and discovered they were based only twenty-two miles from our home, so we attended their next rehearsal in a prison social club hall.

After that, we attended regularly. I was an experienced dancer and learnt quickly, which pleased Beatrice, one of the tutors. The Morris teachers, known as "foremen" or "forepersons," were talented dancers and musicians. They emphasised presentation and our rehearsals were energetic and intense, which showed in our performances. We also discovered that Beatrice was a holistic therapist like myself, and Robert worked within a legal profession closely linked to Paul's occupation.

At practice, Beatrice and Robert explained that our Morris team were the first gothic "side," a term used in the Morris world for "team." When other gothic sides came along, they would add a bit of colour to their costumes so their teams had a different identity. They also said Morris dancing was not a Pagan practice, although many assume it is. Centuries ago, dancers blacked their faces with soot, as black is the only colour that can disguise facial features. The reason for this disguise was so their employers would not recognise them when they performed to top up their wages. They also turned their coats inside out so that they could not be easily identified by their clothes. The coat linings were often torn, so Morris tatters represent this. Morris dancers still uphold these ancient traditions, except for the men darkening their faces, which in this case has been misunderstood as a racially insensitive gesture in recent years.

I enjoyed wearing all black within the Morris team, and the rest of my clothes followed suit. I recently discovered my great paternal grandmother wore only black, which scared the local children. I had transformed from the 'mini-skirted, stiletto-heeled image of my glamour modelling days into something darker and more powerful. Paul looked fabulous in black as he was a handsome man with a muscular build. I tried to encourage him to wear it more often, but frustratingly he preferred beige shorts and khaki coloured t-shirts similar to those worn by his parents and sisters.

My first public performance was outside a small country inn six months later. Fortunately, the audience was small, which lessened the pressure a little. Paul didn't think he'd be a good dancer, but with regular practice and counting while stepping, he performed well.

Ruben joined us at all our practices, sitting to the side with his school homework while we rehearsed. He noticed mistakes during the men's dances, and we realised he had memorised the moves. Ruben also maintained a good rhythm on a drum during his break from homework. I created a Morris kit for him, and he became the first child to join the side as a miniature Morris man. Robert and Beatrice did not usually allow children to participate in the dances, but they made an exception for him because they saw his budding talent and eagerness to perform.

Tammy's unhealthy relationship with a teenage boy from school became even more intense. I discovered she had set up an altar to practise magic in her room, and she may have cast spells to increase the intensity, which concerned us and their teachers at school. They talked all night on the phone, and played truant from school. I attempted to reverse any spells she may have cast, but when I researched the subject, I realised there was nothing I could do but let the magic run its course. After seeing many teenagers use magic for mainly selfish or destructive reasons with no foresight, I understood why the Pagan Federation had an age limit for membership. Tammy unexpectedly left home at sixteen to live with her boyfriend and had no contact with me. Her relationship with Paul had deteriorated and I did not know how to resolve it. I became physically ill when she left, and a homoeopath diagnosed symptoms of grief. Using Reiki helped me through this process.

We were still attending meetings with the Egyptian group, but some members were unhappy with the lack of organisation. We would arrive early in the evening and wait for Penelope to search her reference books for a ritual that we could perform. She didn't plan for our meetings, and by the time she had found a ritual and completed the preparations, it was already late in the evening.

Leonard and his partner, Louise, travelled from London and didn't appreciate having to stay so late when they had work the following day. Three other members decided to leave the group. Although I enjoyed Egyptian rituals, I didn't feel we were progressing in the group.

Later, Penelope cancelled our plans to attend the Summer Solstice event at Stonehenge after Paul had altered his work schedule. She also cancelled group meetings frequently and with short notice, so we decided to move on. Leonard and Louise did likewise.

Our Morris tutors, Beatrice and Robert, invited our whole dance team to their Halloween party. They lived in a beautiful Victorian home and prepared their spacious basement for us. We mingled on original slate floors, dined on a massive oak table, and sat by an open fire. Antique standing candelabras dripped wax, forming intricate shapes as the flickering flames filled the gothic room with warm light. Robert and Beatrice were vegetarian, so their buffet did not contain meat products. Some guests were disappointed, but I found out how delicious a vegetarian buffet could be. I discovered through conversations that Robert and Beatrice were also Pagan, but didn't share their personal life openly with others. I later learnt they were initiates of Alexandrian Wicca, a path that appealed to me as it included Egyptian Deities. Sally, another member of our team, was more forthcoming about her involvement within the Pagan scene. She was what some might call a "name-dropper," listing the renowned high priests, priestesses, authors, and witches she knew.

Later in the evening, some team members bobbed for apples in a large iron cauldron filled with water that stood in the centre of the kitchen/diner. Some successfully retrieved an apple using only their mouths and teeth. Beatrice provided towels for the soggy participants.

Paul and I attended our first Pagan Federation Conference in November 1999 at the Fairfield Halls in Croydon. Peter and Tania, the couple we met during the eclipse, were selling their wares. Speakers provided talks in smaller rooms, and there were many stalls selling occult merchandise. I felt like I had entered a different world. Attendees wore Pagan attire and costumes reminiscent of characters from fairy tales and occult movies. I enjoyed being with like-minded people. Although I had been an extremely protective mother, I let Ruben explore, and sensed he would be safe within this environment.

I attended psychic development circles for two years and researched life after death, because I was taught this did not exist. It was during that time that I read a book entitled The Scole Experiment by Grant and Jane Solomon. It documented the experiences of four spiritualists who researched physical phenomena and conducted experiments in Norfolk during 1996.

Paul and I attended the authors' last Scole Seminar in Norfolk, and the venue for this event was their local village hall that stood adjacent to the cottage where the experiments took place. The cottage had a cellar, an ideal space for the experiments, because total darkness was required. Four spiritualists spoke about their experiences and shared photographs and audio recordings of spiritual phenomena. We met Ernie and Shirley, and their friend Patrick, who hosted a psychic development circle about ten miles away from where we lived. They were friendly and I instantly connected with Shirley, so we exchanged contact details and agreed to meet again.

After the seminar, Leonard and Louise visited us, and I told them about The Scole Experiment. They read the small handbook that included instructions on setting up a space for psychic research, and were eager to participate. We had a spare room as Tammy had left home, and I carefully followed the instructions as I prepared it. I covered the windows with a black-out blind, taping the sides down so that no light could get through, and placed a round garden table and chairs in the room. Electronic devices were not used, as they would interfere with the phenomena, so I used a battery-operated music player. I placed large quartz crystals on the table to act as energy conductors. The handbook also suggested using a large glass dome at the centre of the table to store energy generated by spirit activity. These were not easy to find, but after searching, I was able to acquire one. We covered objects on the table with luminous tape, and group members wore glow-in-the-dark wristbands so we could see any movements.

When the room was ready, I placed an advertisement for group members in a Spiritual Scientist magazine. Someone named Mark contacted us to see if he could join. He had studied this subject for thirty years, using infrared photography to capture spiritual images, and electronic voice phenomena to record spirit voices. Paul and I invited him over, and he brought along a photographic portfolio containing evidence of phenomena, as well as documentation from haunted locations and psychic circles.

Mark had photographs of spirit mediums producing ectoplasm while in a trance state. I hadn't seen ectoplasm before, and in some photos, it fell from the medium's mouth like long strips of folded paper. In others, the substance looked like latex gloves dribbling out of the medium's ears, so I was a little sceptical. I recognised one of the spirit mediums pictured as Colin Fry, the host of a regular psychic television show called Sixth Sense. I had once been in the studio audience, and I noticed how the show was edited in some parts to mislead viewers, which disappointed me.

We soon had six members and began our first experiment. We removed unexposed Polaroid prints in the darkness and laid them on the centre table. We used music to raise energy as our mediums reached a trance state and connected with Spirit. When the session ended, I covered the unexposed polaroid prints with a black bag while inserting them into the camera before switching on the lights. I practised this several times beforehand to ensure I did it correctly. I developed these photographs using a camera with a covered lens to avoid recording any images. Intriguing swirls and shapes appeared on the photos that weren't exposed to light.

I received more requests from readers of the Spiritual Scientist magazine to join our circle. We experimented with different types of music, and discovered that the war-time music of Glenn Miller and other Swing bands seemed to produce the most intense phenomena. During one sitting, while the group meditated in the darkness, I opened my eyes and saw swirls of blue light in front of me, as well as a dark silhouette in the shape of what appeared to be head and shoulders, surrounded by a haze of blue light. It appeared to lean over me, studying my face, and I sat very still as it did so. The group saw small flashes of light from different areas of the room, and on one occasion, I observed an orange glow of light between myself and the person next to me, who also saw it. It was as though we were sitting beside a huge fireplace. A white, wax-like substance began to build on the surface of the crystals over the weeks of our experiments, despite there not being any candles in the room. Mark took scrapings from the crystals home to analyse. Unfortunately, his findings were inconclusive. We did however receive some clear voice phenomena from recordings that were made during our sessions.

Our circle continued for two years, but attendance dwindled as our members had busy lives. These experiments require total commitment and consistent attendance, as any change in the group unbalances the energy. We closed the circle, but Mark remained in contact, and to this day, he continues his work and updates me on his discoveries.

– First dance out with the Morris team.

– Ruben miniature
Morris man

– Polaroid experiment
from the Psychical

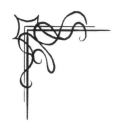

# Chapter 7
## New Discoveries

*March 2000 – October 2000*

I met Lorna in college. She was an attractive woman and a former model like me, with a bubbly personality. She had expressed an interest in Paganism to our tutors, and they suggested she approach me about it. After our first meeting, we developed a close friendship. I worked with the Egyptian deity Sekhmet during dark moon phases, and Lorna joined me for these rituals. She worked with the Goddess Nephthys, who has connections with Sekhmet, and we used menstrual blood in these rituals for potency. Lorna possessed a collection of Egyptian statues, but they were cloistered in a cupboard because her husband insisted that she keep her magical items out of sight.

Lorna had known a spirit medium named Mavis since childhood and praised her abilities, so we planned a clairvoyant evening with her and some of our friends. When Mavis arrived, the smell of tobacco emanated from her. She kept her coat on, explaining that she was always cold from the spirits around her. To prove this, she suggested I hover my hand inches above her knees, and when I did so, it felt as though I'd placed them inside a refrigerator.

Before the event started, Lorna related a time when she hosted a previous clairvoyant evening at her home. Mavis sat quietly with her eyes closed for some time, connecting to Spirit. She opened her eyes suddenly and looked around the room while the group waited in anticipation for a message. Instead, she asked if the host had put the kettle on as she was quite a character!

The messages I received from Mavis were similar to those Alice shared. She mentioned Cornwall, but I wondered if Lorna had divulged some information before-hand. Mavis revealed that my great maternal grandmother had practised witchcraft, and I agreed that was a possibility. My mother had told me that my grandmother thought it was good Romani practice to bow or nod to acknowledge the sun and moon when they were visible. When I stayed overnight at her home, I saw her making ritualistic movements before she got into bed. I asked her what she was doing, and she seemed to be in a trancelike state and didn't hear me. I still remember her bedside lamp. It was a ship, and its sails glowed when she turned it on. Beside the lamp was a box of my grandmother's favourite chocolates in a black box with Black Magic written upon it. She would offer us one before we went to sleep, which was not healthy for our teeth! Many women in my grandmother's generation believed in superstitions and old wives' tales passed down from mother to daughter, and my mother taught me many of them.

Mavis asked me to look deep into her eyes, saying I would recognise her from a previous life. I did as she instructed and sensed a motherly energy, but I wasn't confident enough to say what I felt. She confirmed my thoughts that she was my mother in a past life, who mourned my execution, which matched the reading Alice gave me. I was unsure about this information, but I still felt a connection with Mavis. We spoke on the phone a few times after the event, but we never met in person again.

My Morris team performed the closing ritual at a Beltane event at Conway Hall in June 2000. We practised an intricate dance around a large "Jack"—a tall, dome-shaped wire frame decorated with leaves woven into it that usually contains a person who dances with it. It was a powerful performance where we danced the Gemana, a favourite of mine. This dynamic dance is usually performed by two female dancers, and on this occasion, we had three sets of dancers that performed around the Jack.

Two hundred Pagans formed a circle around us as we danced by candlelight, and as sunglasses were part of our kit, our vision was minimal. Afterwards, each team member pulled a few leaves from the Jack to decorate their hats to bring luck. Perry, one of the male dancers, advised me to keep the leaves until Samhain, and then burn them on a ritual fire.

On the May bank holiday, we performed for three days at our local folk festival where I first saw the Morris team. I enjoyed meeting the rest of the team on a sunny morning outside Robert and Beatrice's Victorian House, surrounded by black iron railings. All team members looked fabulous dressed in their gothic kit. After we had all gathered, we walked through the ancient cobbled streets together. It was early in the morning and the town was quiet, as the dark presence of our

Morris team made their way through the ancient streets. All that could be heard was birdsong and the jingling of male dancer's bells as they walked towards the town. This is one of my favoured memories.

In August 2000, we attended a folk festival in Devon with our Morris team. Our team members camped in tents, but our caravan became a gathering place in the evenings. A few dancers placed their sleeping bags under our awning instead of erecting their tents, but found it rather cold during the night.

One evening, I chatted with a dancer named Sharon about our magical experiences. I was surprised to learn that she and her husband Terry, were members of Robert and Beatrice's coven. Sharon revealed the witch names of all coven members and spoke of sky-clad rituals, unconcerned about the rules of secrecy.

After attending the folk festival, we continued our journey to Cornwall for a vacation and arrived on the day of Lammas. I hoped to find an open ritual to attend, but I hadn't heard of any gatherings. We stayed at Bossiney Camping and Caravan Park to explore the area and discovered a large field opposite the campsite with a pathway leading to a beach. We found a cliff face and coastal path at the far end of the field, and followed this to a slate rock face that we climbed down toward the sea. Paul investigated a waterfall with Ruben, while I sat on the rocks listening to the sea and watching the gulls. I noticed remnants of red candle wax and fragments of left-over strawberries on one of the nearby rocks, which might have been the remains of a Lammas celebration.

I discovered an advertisement for a monthly moot in Bude while reading Pagan Dawn magazine. Paul and I visited this town the following day and found the moot venue at an old inn, but we were three hours early. Ruben was an impatient, hyperactive little boy, and he and Paul didn't want to wait, so we left. During a visit to the Museum of Witchcraft the following day, I overheard a woman conversing with Gary saying how much she enjoyed the moot, and I was disappointed that I couldn't stay.

We had never visited the Cheesewring site at Bodmin before, and to reach it, we had a long walk across the fields against a strong wind. We passed the Nine

Maidens stone circle, and I sensed intense energies when walking through the centre of it. I may have felt more, but was distracted by Ruben protesting about the copious amount of sheep dung we had to trudge through. It was difficult to avoid, and Ruben's facial expression resembled the one he often made while eating vegetables.

Cheesewring is a tower of seven granite slabs stacked on top of each other. The smallest sits at the bottom, the heaviest balance on top, and the entire structure stands thirty-two feet high. With the 'horrors' of the sheep field behind us, Ruben happily climbed the boulders. I placed my hands on the stones and felt the profound spiritual energy that emanated from them. It activated a hunger for more knowledge, and the connection I felt to Cornwall continued to deepen.

I was puzzled by Paul's reluctance to network with the Cornwall Pagan community. While visiting the Witchcraft Museum, I talked with Gary, the owner, for a while, but Paul didn't join us and instead explored the Museum alone. Before we left, I thanked Gary for his time, feeling embarrassed when Paul completely ignored him. Gary's gaze followed him as he left the Museum.

When I joined Paul outside, I asked him why he behaved this way, and he replied that he wanted to create an "air of mystery" about himself. That didn't seem a wise move for someone who planned to move to Cornwall.

When we returned from our vacation, I visited the spiritualist church on the road adjacent to the Kingdom Hall I attended as a child. I have vivid memories of passing it late at night while travelling home in our family car. We saw members of the spiritualist church leaving as my mother made comments about how evil they were. I watched them to see if they appeared odd to prove her claim, and noticed an overweight man standing outside with extremely bushy eyebrows who looked a little intimidating. But otherwise, the others seemed quite ordinary. A small memorial garden across from the church featured an angel statue at its centre that I later discovered was a war memorial. I frequently dreamt of the spiritualist church and the dark gardens opposite. They were imprinted in my mind, so I challenged my mother's fears and experienced their reality.

The church members welcomed me with warmth beneath a full moon. They hosted psychic workshops and development circles. One of the mediums there explained that our personal beliefs did not matter, because the spirit world and the afterlife connected us all, which made sense to me. The service resembled other

Christian churches with hymns and prayers, but only to ensure inclusion on the local church register.

I later attended one of their workshops, where a spirit medium encouraged me to give a psychic message to another person in the group. She handed me ribbons previously held by a member unknown to me, and I shared surprisingly accurate information. A young woman named Vivian invited me to attend a new psychic development circle, to which I told her I would consider it. I hoped she was hosting the circle, but discovered it was someone else. I attended a few times, but it did not last.

Sally was a dancer in my Morris team and a second-degree Gardnerian priestess. She was kind, knowledgeable, and spoke so fast, it was hard to keep up with her. At a dance festival, Sally believed a dancer's injury and ill-health were linked to a psychic attack from a former team member who had a falling out with Beatrice and Robert. They discussed it at length on one of our dance-outs, when Paul received an injury from one of the Morris sticks that split his knuckle. She seemed constantly worried about ill will spells from detractors.

Sally wanted to join Beatrice and Robert's coven, but it was an Alexandrian coven, and they told her if she joined, she would have to start as a beginner. She assumed Gardnerian and Alexandrian paths were the same since Gerald Gardner and Alex Sanders trained in a similar coven. Disappointed, she eventually decided against it.

I asked if I could join them at the same time as Sally, but Robert and Beatrice had wanted to settle Sally into the group before taking on other members. I informed Beatrice I had attained my first degree Reiki qualification and attended a spiritualist church, and her disapproval caught me off guard. She said these were not Pagan practices, but I was in the process of exploring many paths and felt a connection with both healing and Spirit. I couldn't see how they could have a negative impact on my spiritual development.

Sally asked if she could join Lorna and me for our Autumn Equinox celebration, and after discussion, we invited her. We travelled to my in-laws' woodland, and I set up the altar accoutrements on a small table near the stream. I explained the ritual we had planned to Sally, and we added some of her ideas to it.

Darryl, Sally's boyfriend, had joined her. He was a handsome, muscular young male dancer in the Morris team who had a reputation for dating older women. Darryl wasn't Pagan, but had a strong affinity with trees, so he and Paul used this time to trim some of the trees along the woodland path.

When our ritual began, Sally invoked the elementals with her arms out-stretched, and she seemed to transform as her spine curved and she invoked the spirits with a raspy whisper. Lorna and I were mesmerised by this transformation.

During our picnic feast, Sally said she previously worked as a priestess in a coven with Tom, the Scottish Pagan. Their parting wasn't amicable, but she didn't explain why. We discussed planning another ritual celebration, and soon after, Sally suggested forming our own magical group. Beatrice and Robert heard about this decision from Sally and seemed supportive and happy for us.

When we formed our Gardnerian group, there were five members: myself, Lorna, Paul, Sally, and Perry, a male dancer from our Morris group. Darryl attend-ed our group meetings as an assistant, and didn't participate in group practices or rituals.

Our Morris team performed at a Halloween event in London. While we were there, Sally introduced me to some renowned Pagans whom she referred to as her friends. I read about them in Pagan publications and was impressed that Sally knew them and delighted to meet them. Peter and Tania were there with their occult stall, and I introduced them to Sally and updated them on the news concerning our new group. They recommended their Priest Donald if we required one, and Sally replied that she knew him well.

While I watched Galadriel, an alluring belly dancer perform on stage, Robert proudly informed me she was his high priestess, who had initiated him and Beatrice. Sally recently told me a third-degree initiation required the Great Rite, wherein the initiate would have sex with the priest or priestess. I thought about what Robert had said, and curiosity got the better of me, so I asked him outright if he had sex with Galadriel during his third-degree initiation. The rest of the Morris team were nearby and probably heard my question. Robert was shocked, replied that the Great Rite was only for married couples, and left hastily. I later discovered the Great Rite is not obligatory, and could be undertaken by token symbolism of plunging an athame into a chalice, which I was relieved to hear.

Sally advised me to purchase an amber necklace to wear during our magical work, as amber is a powerful stone for dispersing negative energies, so I did. She explained that a second-degree initiate would then wear a necklace of amber and jet, along with a magical ring on the index finger of the right hand and a moon crown. Sally's enthusiasm as she described this filled me with excitement about my future development.

In the evenings I sat at the threshold of our property, watching nature's nighttime activities. I gazed at the dark footpath that led to the woodland and listened to the wind's voice as it whispered through the trees. Bats swooped and circled in groups while Titch, our neighbour's small black cat, sat beside me. I always slept well after spending time out there.

I had read in a book about witchcraft that a glass of water placed under the full moon's rays would energise it, and drinking it would cleanse and energise the body. These practices helped while dealing with life's stressful moments, as well as working on my spiritual development.

– Performance at Conway Halls London

– Dancing at our local Folk Festival

– Ruben and I

– Cheesewring Bodmin

– Spiritualist church

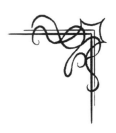

# Chapter 8
## The Gardnerians

*October 2000 – May 2001*

Sally, our group priestess, had a collection of rituals from her former covens stored on her computer, and we chose one for our forthcoming Samhain ritual. We also discussed moon rituals, and Sally said she didn't work with the dark moon, but didn't explain why. She advised me to continue those rituals alone. Lorna no longer celebrated dark moon rituals with me because she had joined our Gardnerian group. Her husband did not want her attending both, as it would mean her spending more time away from home. I was pleased she had not given up magical work altogether and that I still got to see her.

In October 2000, I visited my maternal grandmother's grave on Samhain afternoon to lay flowers, and also harvested pebbles and soil to use in my work. Our first Gardnerian group ritual to celebrate Samhain took place later that evening at my home. Sally brought some of her rituals and altar accoutrements to use, and placed a large cauldron before one of our long low mahogany sideboards we used as an altar. The cauldron contained many circular charcoal blocks, as a thick cloud of incense was required for this ritual.

Sally led the group in a chant to Hecate and Cerridwen for the rebirth of the spirits. As we sang, each group member knelt before the altar to remember their ancestors in the spirit world. We scryed with the incense smoke, looking for the faces of loved ones in the Underworld. Sally's passionate and dramatic invocations, along with the energy we raised, made her body writhe in pleasure. Darryl, her boyfriend, had a dark sense of humour. He sat in the corner observing us, and commented in jest about worshipping Beelzebub while awaiting the feasting and alcohol. I did not feel his presence at our rituals brought positive energy, but said nothing, because he was the partner of our priestess. Otherwise, it was a happy and joyous occasion, and we celebrated afterward with butter-cream and walnut cake, along with a generous amount of red wine.

The altar in our lounge was permanently set up just beneath the staircase. My mother-in-law, May, would occasionally babysit for Ruben, and when I returned home, I would find screwed up sweet-wrappers placed along the edge of the altar. Although Ruben was a child, he had always shown respect for magical items and would not have done this. I sensed it was another attempt from May to let us know she had neither respect nor fear of our beliefs. Ruben once revealed that his grand-mother told him magic was not real and it was all a fantasy, and this supported my suspicions about May.

On one occasion when we returned home, May explained she was sitting alone in the lounge reading a book when she saw a white misty figure float down the stairs and disappear into the wall. I had often heard someone pacing the upper floor when Tammy was late or had stayed out all night. May then blamed her eyesight for the apparition, commenting it was time she had an eye test, but whenever she babysat after that, we would return home to find she had turned on the main lights in all the rooms!

Before our group's next full moon ritual, Sally instructed us to collect personal items from someone we knew who needed protection or healing. Paul and I agreed to construct a talisman for Kevin, my father-in-law, who had cancer and was staying in a hospice. He found it difficult to sleep and calm his mind. I had a small photograph of him, and on a visit to the hospice, I entered his bathroom and retrieved a few strands of his hair from a comb. I added seashells and other personal items to help calm his emotions and send healing energies. Healing energy will work in cases of terminal illness, as it will calm a person throughout their illness, and their eventual death is often a peaceful one.

We melted green candle wax, poured it into a mould, and placed the person-al items into it, along with others connected to peace and healing. Our talismans set quickly in readiness for the ritual work ahead. My home was the primary meeting place for our rituals, and on this night, we raised energy with energetic drumming and chanting from eight o'clock that evening until half-past one the following morn-ing. The next day, our neighbours (who spent more time watching our activities than getting on with their lives) stared into our window as they passed. The smallest of sounds escaped the thin walls of my modern terrace home, so I am sure rumours were circulated about our activities.

Three hours after completing this magical work, the hospice staff contacted May, informing her that Kevin suddenly entered a state of unconsciousness. They asked her to visit as they were unsure of the outcome. May stayed with Kevin and asked Paul to join her that morning. When Paul returned home, he told me Kevin suddenly regained consciousness after eighteen hours. He was alert, happy, and less confused than he was before.

Kevin excitedly attempted to share his extraordinary experience with Paul when May left the room, saying he had "turned a corner." He was about to explain further, but unfortunately, May returned, and he said no more as she would neither believe, nor wish to hear what he had to say. Kevin spoke of his sister and mother, who passed away some time ago, and wished to sort out unfinished business with his family.

After Kevin was diagnosed with cancer, he borrowed my copy of The Scole Experiment by Grant and Jane Solomon, and the scientific experiments involving the afterlife intrigued his atheistic mind. He mentioned in jest that he would take his mobile phone with him and contact me from the spirit world.

I visited Kevin at the hospice and provided manicures, reflexology, and reiki treatments. The difference in temperature during his reiki treatments was remarkable, as Kevin's body felt so cold while I was extremely hot. On one of our visits, he tried to explain a dream he had, unsure whether he was asleep, or between the stages of wakefulness and sleep. He walked through a crowd of people and recognised some of them, but instead of bumping into them, their shoulders passed through his own. May would not have taken this seriously, but I sensed he was connecting with others in the spirit world.

A specific date was arranged for members of Paul's family to visit the hospice. Paul recalled that before Kevin gave his family any information, he lowered his head and closed his eyes. The description of his actions was reminiscent of how spirit mediums work when communicating with the spirit world. Kevin seemed to listen and quietly acknowledge someone that no one else could see before speaking to his family on important matters. Kevin was an atheist throughout his life, and it was wonderful to witness the sudden change in him. When he sorted his financial and relationship matters with his family, he seemed more content, and on my next visit, he calmly told me he was ready to go. Kevin slept peacefully during the next month and was no longer afraid to die. He passed away peacefully at home under the watchful eye of May.

The day he died, I sensed something occurring and asked Paul to contact May, but he was determined to finish his chores first. Within minutes, May called us, concerned Kevin was on the threshold of passing, but Paul did not think it would happen so soon and promised May he would visit as soon as he finished his chores. May contacted us again five minutes later to tell us Kevin had passed away. She lived twenty-two miles from us, so Paul would not have arrived in time, even if he had left immediately.

Yuletide had been difficult for Paul and his family, as Kevin passed away on the nineteenth of December, and his funeral was arranged for January. He had heard me play one of my Morris team's tunes on a button accordion and mentioned he would like it played at his funeral, so we invited them. Our Morris team performed at his wake in his local theatre, where he performed in pantomimes as a member of the amateur dramatics group. Kevin's obituary described him as a fun, loving character who enjoyed the unusual aspects of life.

The final part of the funeral ceremony at their local crematorium will remain in my memory. A vicar, Paul's cousin, spoke about Kevin's life and achievements, and with his closing sentence, he gestured towards the coffin and said, "I give you Kevin," and the curtain slowly closed for the last time with no applause, just silence. His friends and relatives sat in silence for a few minutes observing the closed red curtain, but I could still hear the cheering, applause, and standing ovations he received after his performances. I will never forget Kevin's lively, amusing character, and the abundance of affection he gave to Tammy and me when we needed it most.

Sally thought our development within the Gardnerian group had progressed quicker than expected, and was pleased with our work. She visited Beatrice and Robert regularly to update them on her group's success, and suspected they were having problems with members of their coven. Sally assumed they were jealous of her group, but added that rivalry between covens is traditional.

I planned to attend the Pagan Conference in London with Beatrice and Robert. We had offered to transport Sally, but she decided to travel by train with Darryl. As we arrived at the venue, we noticed Sally and Darryl walking towards it soaked from the falling rain. Shortly after, I heard a talk by an unusual speaker in robes and recognised him as Arthur Pendrake. I heard he was arrested for intoxication and spent a night or two in the police cells, where he proceeded to knight the police officers with a sword.

I explored the stalls alone after Pendrake's talk and eventually met Sally, who ignored me when I approached her. Puzzled by this reaction, I asked for an explanation, and she expressed how upset she was that we had transported Beatrice and Robert to the conference while allowing our high priestess to walk in the rain. I reminded Sally we offered her transport to the venue, but she declined. She expected to hear I would be leaving her group to join Beatrice and Robert's coven, given we gave them a lift to the conference and not her. It concerned me that she had made these assumptions without discussing the situation. Sally informed me that high priestesses expect to be chauffeured from their homes by group members to Pagan events and have their bags carried for them while they are there.

To allay her fears, I accompanied Sally for the rest of the day, and when we attended the next talk, I offered her the only empty chair and sat on the floor beside her. I carried her bag and did all I could to assist, which pleased her. No other group members attended the conference, so the responsibility was all mine.

I met former members of Sally's magical groups from the Bristol area who commented on how well she looked. She introduced me to Donald, a handsome priest who often had an entourage of young admiring female witches. Sally informed me Donald had agreed to work with our group when required. A beloved professor whom I admired and whose books I had read kissed my hand and said it was an honour to meet me. It was exciting to meet renowned Pagans, and it impressed me that Sally knew them.

Not long after the conference, I purchased a book entitled Covencraft by Amber K to research the requirements of coven members and their responsibilities toward priestesses. I found nothing on this subject and discussed my experiences at the conference with Lorna, who disagreed with group members having to behave like servants. I thought about this from an alternative perspective: a priestess and priest give up their time to train members of their group, so assisting them would be a way of acknowledging and appreciating the work they do. I heard revelations from other Pagan women who unknowingly joined abusive covens and considered myself fortunate that our group seemed to be progressing well. Sally did not mention the incident at the conference again.

Our group arranged to discuss a forthcoming full moon ritual. Sally asked each of us to research a deity to whom we felt connected. At the ritual, she instruct- ed us to take our deity's spirit into our bodies to "become" them, and reveal more information about them by introducing our deity to the group. Pagan friends of ours thought it far too early in our development to take on such a task, but we followed her instructions carefully, and it seemed to go well.

Paul and I had a disagreement the following day, and he blamed the deity I invoked and assumed I held onto its energy. He seemed uncomfortable with the presence of Sekhmet in our home and anything associated with her. Paul had heard Penelope explaining that Sekhmet did not like men, so this may have been a reason. On reflection, I believe Penelope also sensed his dislike of Sekhmet during our time within the Egyptian group considering the advice she eventually gave me.

Beatrice and Robert invited Paul and me to their Yuletide party with other members of our Morris team. Sally had arranged to spend the weekend elsewhere, and seemed a little uncomfortable when she heard we accepted their invitation.

When we arrived, Beatrice offered to take my coat to the bedroom, and I noticed her studying some loose hairs on it as she walked away. I wonder now if she kept a few strands for spellwork. When she returned, I asked out of curiosity if it would be appropriate for me to see their temple, and Beatrice replied by immediately escorting me there. I followed her up four flights of stairs to the attic room in their beautiful townhouse. Beatrice bowed at the altar, and I followed her lead. Then I stood back to take in the surroundings, gazing at the pale green walls that backdropped an image of Isis and Osiris above the altar. Clean, highly polished magical tools glinted in the low light. A large antique brass oil lamp with a green glass chimney dangled from the sloped ceiling, and a church candle perpetually glowed from within a tall cylindrical red glass holder. I commented on the welcoming atmosphere and wished I had space to create a permanent temple space, because it was hard work to prepare the lounge for each group meeting. After a while, we rejoined the gathering in their kitchen, and as we did so, I noticed her nod towards Robert as they exchanged glances.

Sally suffered from a severe external health problem that stressful situations would aggravate. She believed it was caused by a hex directed at her by a former coven acquaintance. Though we were working together, we hadn't yet become initiated as a coven. I expected a coven priestess to be strong in mind and set an example for her group, which cast doubts on my desire to be initiated by her. Sally would receive a euphoric high during our rituals and absorb the energy the group generated.

When she met her friends at events, they commented on how radiant and healthy she looked since she began running our group.

Beatrice and Robert visited us one evening, and although I did not want to be disloyal, I voiced my concerns about the Gardnerian group. They confirmed I was right to doubt how Sally had acted with her group, and they were concerned that some of her teaching methods were questionable. Sally impulsively moved from place to place without warning, and stated she would move away if her relationship with Darryl ended, which did not give our members security within the group.

Lorna enjoyed participating in rituals, and the magical work came naturally to her, but her attendance at our group meetings dwindled. Lorna's husband had been curious about her magical path and read a book she purchased entitled The Witch's Bible by Janet and Stewart Farrar. He asked if she really wanted to involve herself in the type of religion where some "dirty old man" would have her strip naked for initiation and his pleasure. After hearing this conversation, it did not surprise me that Lorna's attendance was less frequent.

Sally's birthday was imminent, and although Paul had decided he would leave the group, he postponed doing so until after her birthday celebration. I constructed a new hand-stitched robe for her, and although she seemed pleased and it fitted her perfectly, I saw her examine the stitching while we were feasting. I had witnessed her being overly critical in other situations and wondered what she thought of the gift, but she said nothing negative.

A few days after the group meeting for Sally's birthday, the time arrived to give her news of Paul's departure. He refused to tell her himself and left that responsibility to me. Sally was understandably upset and pleaded with me to stay in the group as she was aware of my eagerness to learn, which placed me in an awkward position.

Lorna also contacted Sally to let her know she could not continue her membership with the group as she had too many commitments. I knew this would change the group dynamics, so I also decided to leave, as Paul would not have allowed group rituals to continue within our home.

Our decision to leave created tension during Morris team rehearsals. Sally didn't attend the next practice, so I gave her magical accoutrements to Darryl, who closely observed our interaction with Beatrice and Robert. Their coven members also left their group, as they found the training too restrictive, and described them as their "moral guardians who watched every move." I was surprised to hear this, as I thought them fortunate to be in such a well-structured coven.

Beatrice contacted me by telephone to tell me that Sally had visited her. The reason she gave for Paul leaving was his inability to follow a woman's instructions. She said I had left because of emotional problems that required professional help, which amused Beatrice, considering Sally's state of mind. I heard through Peter and Tania that Donald, the priest who Sally said would work with our group, told them he wouldn't work with her again as she had a long history of mental health problems. This confirmed we had made the right decision to leave, but I have many positive memories of our time together, despite the problematic moments.

Unaware that I had heard about her conversation with Beatrice, Sally continued to contact me as though nothing had changed. Still, my main concern was maintaining a good atmosphere within the Morris team. Perry, the last group member, continued to work magically with Sally and would not comment on the situation, as it was the correct way to handle it. Beatrice and Robert advised us to wait at least six months before joining another magical group, and I understood their reasoning as Sally closely observed our interaction with them. We hoped that in time, this awkward situation would settle.

A few weeks passed before Sally left the Morris team, and I no longer heard from her. She gave Beatrice and Robert no reason for her departure, but she once confessed to me that she coveted Beatrice's life. Everything seemed to turn out right for her, and Sally couldn't understand why everything in her own life went wrong. Her relationship with Darryl ended, and she moved to London, so the tension within the Morris team subsided.

Beatrice stayed away from Morris practices for a while, as she had grown tired of teaching members. I understood how frustrating it would be to train strong dancers only for them to leave, and then have to begin again with new recruits. I offered to help and took on the responsibility of the teacher, where I discovered how challenging it could be.

On May Day 2001, we performed on Bluebell Hill for a yearly ceremony. Local Morris teams gather for this event before sunrise, and the celebrations begin with a song entitled Jack in the Green. We all join in with the chorus, and then each Morris team performs their dances. It takes a lot of effort to get up early and dress in Morris kit at that time of the morning, but it is worth it to experience the atmosphere and energy of this event. The haunting sight of Morris dancer's tatters in-flight, shrouded in the morning mist to the heavy heartbeat of a drum, is something to behold! Beatrice left the group momentarily to wash her face in the morning dew, which I discovered is an ancient practice for women to retain their youth and beauty.

Paul often stated that I should be more like him, stronger in mind and positive about life. Since we weren't working in any magical groups, I suggested a joint meditation, and the first attempt was unsuccessful. I understood that he did not want overwhelming structure in other aspects of his life due to his highly disciplined occupation. We tried a second time while sitting cross-legged on the floor facing one another and joined hands. We meditated for a while, and Paul later revealed that he saw my image, which transformed into a large book during his meditation. The book opened, and the pages began to turn quickly, making a fluttering sound. The pages turned into the wings of a bird that hovered in front of him for a while before flying away. I did not realise how significant this would be in the future.

– The Gardenarian Altar for Yule

– Me outside the Witchcraft Museum 2001

– Morris team performing outside the Witchcraft Museum 2001

# Chapter 9
## Handfasting

*June 2001*

Paul and I discussed having a Handfasting ceremony in Cornwall. We were legally married in a register office eleven years earlier through a formal process devoid of spirituality. My mother and father attended, as it was not in a church other than their own, along with Paul's family and friends. During the 'father of the bride' speech, my dad picked up his Bible and began reading scriptures about marriage being a "three-fold cord." He stated that if Paul and I included God in our relationship, it would be stronger. My father chose to do this instead of the usual way that fathers talk about their daughters, sharing special memories, as fathers usually do at weddings. We didn't want the occasion to be religious, so I was embarrassed about this, and Paul's friends didn't appreciate it either.

Since Paul and I seemed to share the same spiritual view, I wanted to bless our marriage in a meaningful way. Paul's friends were atheists, and it was a ceremony my parents would not attend, but as it was personal to us, we discussed it with Beatrice and Robert. They agreed to be our celebrants, and we began to make plans.

Our 2001 family vacation started with a day of dance with our Morris team in Devon and concluded with our handfasting ceremony in Cornwall on the twelfth of June. This date also marked the fiftieth anniversary of the repeal of the Fraudulent Mediums Act of 1951 and the end of all the anti-witchcraft legislation that came before it. Along with Beatrice and Robert, members of our Morris team attended to support us, which meant a lot, since our families and friends had shown no interest. We had given the Museum of Witchcraft advance warning of our intention to perform there to mark the anniversary of the repeal.

Paul purchased a Volkswagen camper van from Bella, the young woman I met while attending my first Pagan moot. Unfortunately, the van broke down during its first journey, and one of our dancers towed it home, so we used the car instead. After we returned from our trip, Paul contacted Bella, who refused to take the camper van back and give Paul a refund, since it was beyond repair. Paul and Darryl then took the van back to her and sped away in our car before she could object.

We had no tent when we arrived at the Devon Day of Dance, so Paul attached the camper van awning to our car to provide shelter that night. It was an extremely cold night, and I could not generate enough body warmth in the awning to sleep, so I moved to the car. After the day of dance, we travelled to Tintagel, Cornwall. Paul hired a static caravan at a site opposite Bossiney Camping and Caravan Park, where the rest of our Morris team stayed.

Rhonda had advertised for penfriends in Pagan Dawn magazine, and I corresponded with her for a few months. She arranged to travel to Cornwall from her home in Wales to attend our Handfasting ceremony. Rhonda's letters had been long and full of personal detail, but the conversation was minimal in person. She was completely different in personality and appearance than I imagined her to be.

The day after her arrival, we were eager to take our Morris team to St. Nectan's waterfall. Beatrice and Robert could then survey the area we chose for the handfasting ceremony as our celebrants. Our team were fit and fast on their feet, so we quickly made our way through the Glen. In my eagerness to reach the waterfall, I hadn't realised Rhonda had difficulties keeping up with us. Gasping for breath with a bright red face, she sat on a rock to rest for a moment. I returned for her, and when I passed Perry, he jokingly asked if I was attempting to "kill her off!" Rhonda later commented that her trip to Cornwall had confirmed she needed to lose weight and improve her fitness.

We performed outside the King Arthur's Arms in Tintagel that evening, where I offered to buy Rhonda a drink. She requested a straight brandy, and surprised me when instead of slowly savouring it, she drank it immediately as though it were a shot.

The male members of our Morris team performed a favourite dance of mine where Beatrice usually stood in the centre playing a haunting tune on her melodeon while the men danced around her. On special occasions, the team places a person or something of significance in the centre, and this time they placed Paul and me there while they danced around us. I heard the occasional squeal from Paul when the male dancers poked and punched him as they passed.

We enjoyed a wonderful evening and returned to the campsite rather late.

Two of our new female members had to complete playful initiation tasks as our Morris men had the humour of school boys when we went away for performances. Darryl brought a large bottle of scrumpy, and when he offered Rhonda a drink from the bottle, he claimed she returned it half empty. It seemed Rhonda could drink most of the Morris men under the table.

The following day on the twelfth of June, we performed outside the Museum of Witchcraft on a warm and sunny afternoon. We were surprised the Museum hadn't organised any other events for this special anniversary. Still, our Morris team were delighted to have an opportunity to dance on this momentous occasion. On arrival, we walked in procession towards the museum to the solitary beat of our drum. The residents and a few tourists stopped to observe us, and Gary, the Museum owner, was excited to hear us in the distance, knowing we were on our way. He was once a Morris dancer and concertina player who loved anything associated with folk music. The spectators enjoyed our performance, and nine-year-old Ruben performed with the male dancers. Rhonda was delighted to witness this, and found it an emotional experience. We invited Gary to our Handfasting, and he politely declined, but gave us a wonderful gift of two mano cornuto charm pendants for protection from the museum shop.

The retail outlet owners opposite the museum were unhappy about its presence and often displayed anti-witchcraft flyers in their shop. Robert told me that Beatrice strode into the shop wearing her leather jacket with a huge pentacle on the back, and the shop assistant's eyes widened at the sight of this. When Paul and I returned a few days after the performance, Gary was excited by the reaction it caused from the Christian community, as they arranged for the church choir to sing hymns the next day in the space where we performed.

It was a dry, cloudy evening when we prepared to visit St. Nectan's waterfall for our Handfasting ceremony. Paul paid a reasonable price for the hire of the site and a buffet prepared by the owners. Ben, the site owner, offered to transport Beatrice, Robert, Perry, and me along the back road to the waterfall with our altar table and accoutrements. As I emerged from the car and walked towards the entrance gate, I received a wonderful surprise when Lorna, her son, and her mother arrived to join us. I knew they were in Cornwall for their vacation, but I didn't expect to see them, as it was quite a distance from Tintagel.

I entered the meditation shrine to change into my Handfasting attire while Beatrice, Robert, and Perry took the altar and accoutrements down to the waterfall and set up the space. They purchased fresh flowers to construct a Handfasting crown and decorate our besom. I stood at the granite altar, finding it hard to believe my wishes were coming true, and I thanked the spirits for their assistance in making it all possible. Lorna stood beside me, and she was concerned I would smudge my eye makeup as we experienced an emotional moment together.

Before we left for Cornwall, Paul had upset Beatrice when they came to discuss the final arrangements. He announced that he and Robert would discuss the important things in another room and leave the ladies to converse about the wedding dress. I recall Beatrice looking at me, shocked that Paul would suggest this. As I stood at the altar in my gown, Beatrice came and went, making preparations. She did not mention my dress, and I sensed by her silence that she had not forgotten Paul's words.

Meanwhile, Paul made his way through the glen with the rest of the Morris team. This took a while, as they had a supply of ale with them. After their arrival, we slowly descended the steep slate steps to the waterfall. As we reached the bottom, we saw Beatrice and Robert standing by a beautiful altar, surrounded by candlelight. Two long fallen trees displayed a row of tea light candles, and created a magical pathway to the altar that took my breath away.

All the Morris team members stood outside the sacred space on a higher ledge of the rock face to observe the ceremony while Rhonda stood behind me and held my bouquet beside Lorna and her mother. Ruben wanted to join us in the circle, but one of the team members held him back as they were concerned he may be disruptive. I now wish he had stood with us. Beatrice and Robert conducted the handfasting beautifully and were warm, friendly, and helpful. I had memorised my words for the ceremony, but Paul referenced Beatrice and Robert's Book of Shadows, which Perry held for us.

Just before the ceremony began, a kingfisher flew across the space, and after Beatrice closed the circle, two small birds flew around the perimeter of it together and then flew away. Beatrice tied our wrists together with a short, thin red cord as they had not mentioned we could have supplied our own and she instructed us to remain this way for the rest of the evening. This brought back memories of the joint "stag and hen night" before our legal wedding when Paul's friend "ball and chained" our ankles together for the evening. My ball was light, but Paul's was filled with concrete. We had to go everywhere together, even when visiting the bathrooms in nightclubs.

After the ceremony, we spent the evening in the refreshment area where Ben and Jill had prepared a sumptuous buffet. Darryl was a talented artist and decorated our cake with Celtic symbols using an icing pen. The wedding party feasted, played the drums, and sang until late in the evening. When it was time to leave, Paul forcibly removed his hand from the cord as we sat in the car, saying he could not drive while we were tied together. While making the arrangements for our Handfasting and during the festivities, I sensed he wasn't too enthusiastic about it, but went through with it to please me. This is one of many examples of how he would go out of his way to give me what I wanted out of love.

Perry mentioned he no longer worked magically with Sally, but they conversed by email. He said how much he enjoyed working in a sacred space with us again during the ceremony, and I replied that I planned to approach Robert and Beatrice again about joining their coven. Perry said he was also reviewing his spiritual path. We returned to the campsite where the celebrations continued.

I invited Rhonda to stay with us overnight, as I had spent little time with her. This may not have been wise, as it was our wedding night, though we were not newlyweds and Ruben was also with us. She explained that she didn't have enough money to buy us a handfasting gift, which I told her not to worry about. We purchased drinks for her, and I gave her a bracelet as a gift. She also saved some money on accommodation by staying the night with us.

The next day, she proudly showed me an expensive statue of Isis that she purchased in Boscastle. Paul was upset by this, and it provided further ammunition for his belief that Pagans were out to exploit others.

# Chapter 10
## Initiation

June 2002 – December 2002

Although Paul was involved in the Pagan scene, I sensed he was not completely comfortable within it. Our non-Pagan friends excluded us from their dinner parties, as Paul had acquired a "ready-made family," and his circle of friends had no children at this time. They also frowned upon Paul's involvement in Paganism and Morris dancing, but they had begun to exclude us anyway before we became involved in these groups. Paul liked to generate gossip amongst them about his unusual interests because he enjoyed the attention.

A month after our Handfasting, we arranged to visit Beatrice and Robert to discuss joining their Alexandrian coven. I knew Sally had feared this all along, but I respected them for their discipline as Morris teachers, and also needed to learn the Craft within a well-structured, secure group. They asked us questions about our level of commitment and our past experiences in magical groups, and as they were satisfied with our answers, they agreed to take us on as members. Paul only agreed to join the coven, as Beatrice would not accept me without him, since the group required a balance of male and female energy.

Terry and Sharon, their two former initiates, were given another chance to return, but declined the invitation, as their lifestyle was seemingly rather promiscuous. They were known for hosting wild parties, and invited other members of the Morris team to them. Paul and I politely declined their invitations, as he had told me we had to be careful of our conduct due to the status of his position within the police force. Terry once referred to Beatrice and Robert as his "moral guardians," and from what I witnessed, he and Sharon had no intention of changing this aspect of their lives. After conversing with them, it seemed they were physically attracted to Beatrice and Robert, and hoped that joining their coven would make their relationship more intimate. When it did not turn out as they hoped, it seemed they lost interest.

Beatrice and Robert gave us specific preparation instructions. Our athames, a Pagan word for dagger, were to be exorcised. To begin, we buried them in the earth under the willow tree in our garden for two weeks. When we dug them up to retrieve them, the earth had shifted, and the athames had moved from their original position, so it took a while to find them.

We then had to exorcise them in fire and water by heating up the blade in a candle flame until it was black and then plunge it into a bowl of water a certain number of times. I remember the satisfying hiss of the blade as it hit the water. When that was completed, we painted Wiccan symbols along the length of our athame handles and blessed them with incense.

We already owned black robes without hoods, so we purchased some black material to attach hoods to them. The needlework was left to me, as Paul had no desire or skill with a needle and thread. Acquiring the four red cords that were nine feet in length was easy, as we purchased them at a haberdashery stall.

During one of our Morris events, Beatrice delightedly told me that Perry had asked to join the Alexandrian coven. I was also delighted to hear this, as I had enjoyed working magically with him, and he had handled the awkward situation with Sally tactfully and considerately.

There were further problems within the Morris team, disagreements and political issues that I attempted to distance myself from, which was difficult at times while working close together. Still, I continued to focus on performance and teamwork, and offered to take on the squire position after being a team member for only six weeks. A teenage girl who was assigned the role had a disagreement with Beatrice at the Whitby folk festival, and this ended with her departure on our return. This role required arranging the order of performances at festivals by conversing with other squires from various Morris teams. I also continued in the role of foreperson, teaching dances to the female Morris team.

We performed at the first Lammas Festival in Eastbourne and attended their seasonal ritual on a full moon. Eastbourne is well known for being a place where people go to retire, and it was the first time the organisers had conducted a ritual on the beach there. Members of the public paused to observe, and some were laughing as they watched Pagans in robes holding staffs, casting circles, and invoking the elementals while singing and chanting.

After this event, Paul and I travelled to Cornwall for three days to meet with Peter and Tania at the Battle of Camlann re-enactment. It was another wonderful opportunity to sit by the sea, listening to voices within the waves, and connecting with the elements. Breathing the clean air while listening to the gulls is sublime, and when I experience this, there is nowhere else I would rather be. The energy from the Atlantic Sea in Eastbourne has a completely different energy from the Cornish Ocean, and I did not feel the same connection there.

We visited the Museum of Witchcraft and conversed with Gary, the owner, about our handfasting ceremony as he browsed the photographs in our album. I observed how gently and carefully he turned the pages. He treated the album with the utmost respect, providing a glimpse of how he handled the museum artefacts.

Beatrice and Robert returned to Tintagel for a vacation in June, when there were less children around. Other members of our Morris team enjoyed their time there with us, and also returned during the summer to explore more of the area.

Paul, Ruben, and I visited a beach at Crackington Haven, and discovered an abundance of hag stones and phallic-shaped grey stones covered in white markings. We collected some as gifts for Pagan friends to place upon their altars, and my female friends were impressed with them. I still have one that I place on the windowsill to keep my bathroom window ajar.

On our return home, Paul and I discussed our forthcoming initiation into the coven. I felt a little unsettled about being "sky-clad," a Pagan term for "naked." In the past, I had worked as a photographic glamour model and attended a naturist club, but this situation was completely different, as I would have little control over it. I had worked sky-clad during solitary magical practice though, and this felt free, comfortable, and natural.

Paul and I were initiated on the same evening, but were prepared in separate rooms before we were individually guided to the temple. Beatrice and Robert instructed us to arrive at their home immediately after bathing, wearing no chemicals, deodorant, perfume, or cosmetics, so we were as clean as the day we were born. I felt truly naked, as I was unaccustomed to leaving the house without facial cosmetics and wearing my favourite perfume. We brought our freshly laundered robes, cords, a scarf for a blindfold, athame, and some flowers for the altar.

I went into a room, removed all my clothes, and waited. There was a shawl draped over the back of a chair that I draped over my lap, as I felt exposed. Beatrice entered the room, tied my hands with cords, and covered my eyes with a blindfold. I felt vulnerable as I sat alone on the chair in Beatrice's holistic treatment room. Before she left me, I felt her lift the shawl from my lap as though she were looking beneath it, but she did not remove it. I heard her walk to the door, and there was a silent pause before she left the room. The lack of movement and vision heightened my senses, and I became aware of an energy that felt like long, spindly elemental fingers that crept up my body from my feet to my head. I now realise that this was a visit from an elemental spirit who had been watching my development and was awaiting the time when I would be ready to connect with it after another eight years had passed.

I heard pacing and chanting from the temple above me as the coven raised energy. Beatrice returned to retrieve me, and proceeded to gently guide me up two flights of stairs to the temple above. Before entering the temple, I felt the sharp pressure of the coven sword on my chest as I was instructed to reveal the password. I felt Robert behind me as he pressed his naked body against mine, and Beatrice did the same in front of me, so that I was sandwiched between them and pushed into the temple. I felt such intensity from everything that was done within the ritual; some parts I felt quite comfortable with, while other aspects I found a little disturbing. After the initiation ritual, when my bonds were released and the blindfold removed, I felt a change within myself, and the sights of my surroundings were more intense. Robert brought Paul to the temple, and when he appeared, I noticed that the cords around his wrists had been re-wound awkwardly, and held in the original position to give the impression that he was still bound. I saw Beatrice glance at the ropes, and wondered if she noted this as his resistance to being in a submissive situation.

After our initiation, Paul and I travelled forty-four miles each week to visit Beatrice and Robert, as we were required to copy, by hand, the words from their coven Book of Shadows. Beatrice and Robert had copied their book from their high priestess, Galadriel, and she had copied hers from the original Book of Shadows created by Alex Sanders. So as we created our copies, we could trace them back three steps directly to him.

We sat at their kitchen table and copied two or three of the ninety-nine pages on each visit. There was an occasion when I visited alone, as Paul had to work, and on my return home, he copied the pages from my book. During the next session, we both began copying from the same page, and Beatrice commented that Paul had not reached that page. He explained he had copied the previous pages from my book, but she replied we were only permitted to copy words from the coven Book of Shadows. Beatrice had him return to that page and copy it out again. I understood the reason for this, as any mistakes I could have made would have been copied by him, but this annoyed Paul.

Whenever I visited Beatrice and Robert's home, it was extremely quiet, as they had no music playing, did not own a television, and the only sounds were the ticking and chiming of their antique clocks. The decor in their home complimented the Victorian building, and it was rather like travelling back in time during our visits. Paul sat there with his arms folded, and his eyes shifted from side to side in the silence, and when he could bear it no more, he rambled on about what was going on in his life. Beatrice smiled and said, "You can't handle silence, can you?" Paul didn't have much to say in response to that.

On the occasions I visited them alone, Beatrice would sit opposite me at the table in silence with a smile on her face, and I would smile back at her. I was quite happy to sit there without conversing, although it was reminiscent of the method used by psychiatrists who sit quietly waiting for their clients to speak. Beatrice had attained a degree in psychology, which meant she would also be aware of this method, and it would give her insight into others' personalities based on their reactions to it.

Our training within the coven progressed, but I sensed Perry felt a little guilty about leaving Sally. Paul attempted to take shortcuts during his training, which did not create a good impression or do him any favours. There also seemed to be a little jealousy surfacing within our coven, as Paul thought Perry the favoured member. Perry had known Beatrice and Robert for many years, and during his initiation, I heard Robert tell him they had waited seven years for that moment.

When Beatrice discovered I attended Yoga classes, she invited me to one of her local advanced sessions run by a couple she knew. Many Yoga teachers attended this class, as it challenged their abilities. I was flexible in body, and enjoyed challenging postures such as the lotus pose.

Beatrice said that her hips were not as flexible as mine, and she commented that she would not even try this posture. She told me that she was better at inverted postures. Beatrice could accomplish a headstand very well, particularly the part where she placed her head on the ground first, then raised her feet slowly from the floor with her legs straight until they were in an upright position. This move requires strong abdomen and arm muscles when raising the legs. As much as I tried, it was a move I could not manage, so at the beginning of each session, Beatrice would perform this move in front of me, while I watched in fascination.

This was one aspect that revealed her competitive nature. The tutors tried to persuade her to become a Yoga teacher, but at this time, she was not interested in doing so. Years later, however, Beatrice had a change of mind, and chose to take on the role.

When Tammy left home, it was her choice to have no contact with us for eighteen months, because we disapproved of her troublesome boyfriend. This was a difficult time for me, and my Reiki self-treatments, energy exercises known as Hat-surei Ho, and meditations helped me through it. We eventually heard from her, and discovered that she lived in her own apartment. Paul was the first to visit in order to assess the situation, and then I accompanied him to see her. I walked into her apartment and saw a five month old baby boy lying on a play-mat kicking his legs. I immediately picked him up, and he looked at me, puzzled, not knowing who I was. It was a strange feeling to realise that I had become a grandmother during my thirties!

Tammy received an unexpected visit from my parents to see their great-grand-child. While they were there, my mother warned her against witchcraft, expressing how dangerous and detested by God it is. My mother assumed that I would encourage my children to follow this path in the same way she insisted we followed her religion. I chose not to raise my children in any religion, as I did not want to put them off. I advised them to do their own research and choose the path that resonated with them.

Members of our Morris team soon worked out that we were in Beatrice and Robert's coven when they overheard them greet us with "Blessed Be." Our closer relationship with them, along with taking on the role of officers within the Morris team, changed our relationship with other members who seemed to distance themselves from us. One of the first Morris parties we attended revealed the group were not relaxed while Beatrice was there, and they described it as having their school headmistress present. Beatrice and Robert eventually left, because the loud music gave Robert a headache, and once gone, the group relaxed and the party came to life. Ruben spent a lot of time with the male dancers and had memorised their risqué songs. These amused him, even though at nine years of age, he didn't fully understand the lyrics. We later discovered he sang these songs at school, when the teacher wrote a comment on his end-of-year report about how he often entertained the class with his colourful songs. Ruben appeared confident and outspoken during performances with the Morris team, as he associated mainly with adults.

Some of the members thought Ruben rather precocious and undisciplined, but I had intentionally raised him to be a confident child so he did not become a target for abusers who could ruin his childhood. I was also a firm parent when needed, as Paul, besotted with his son, would not refuse him anything. He would not allow Ruben to hear constructive criticism, and this affected Ruben during adolescence and adulthood, when he found it difficult to handle criticism from other sources.

I continued to teach the dances as a foreperson for the women. Their strong personalities remained a challenge, but I understood that Beatrice and Robert needed to delegate roles, as they had other pressures and responsibilities. I hoped the situation within the team would improve, as I did not see myself continuing as foreperson for long, and sensed this would cause further problems.

The Morris team were once again asked to perform at the Halloween Festival, and while the team waited near the entrance to process into the main hall, I met a beautiful female singer by the name of Claire Von Trane. It was the first time I had seen Claire and heard her music on a small compact disc player by her stall. I purchased one of her albums after a short conversation with her, and on returning home, I noticed her telephone number was displayed on the reverse side of the cover. After listening to Claire's album, I sent a mobile phone text giving positive feedback, and to my surprise, she answered immediately. I arranged for her to visit me, and found her a gentle, friendly person, so a friendship naturally developed between us. Claire's voice was rather unique, but not to everyone's taste, as Paul asked me not to play her music while he was around. Claire explained to me she had acquired this unique singing style during trance meditation, and I was astounded by the loud powerful voice that emanated from such a tiny woman!

Before Claire entered the Pagan scene, she was a vocalist for rock bands, and had also recorded a song for the opening scene of a popular movie. The young man she cohabited with did not support her new style of singing. However, I admired Claire's talent and enjoyed spending time with her. I listened to her unusual views on certain aspects of life and enjoyed having a singer in my life again, as I missed Tammy's beautiful operatic voice after she left home. Paul described Claire as a haughty person, and I understood why she could appear that way, but she was also a loving, caring and good-hearted friend. When I mentioned to Beatrice that Claire and I had developed a closer friendship, it surprised her. I did not know that Galadriel, Beatrice's high priestess, also had a close friendship with her.

During our coven meetings, Beatrice and Robert gave us books to read and asked us to share our thoughts on those that resonated with us. The Pickingill Papers by W.E. Lidell fascinated me. It details the life of cunning-man George Pickingill, and includes accounts about shape shifting from residents in his village. Witnesses have claimed to have seen thirteen white hares in the graveyard, which corresponded with the same number of members in Pickingill's coven. These stories intrigued me. Choosing this book surprised Beatrice; she didn't expect me to connect with the Cunning Craft and peasant magic, as Alexandrians were into high ceremonial practice. Paul enjoyed The Triumph of the Moon by Ronald Hutton, and Beatrice and Robert also spoke highly of it.

Perry, Paul, and I prepared the temple with Robert's assistance before our coven rituals. Beatrice had also given me a recipe for mooncakes, and I watched her make them on one occasion. After that, they were my responsibility. I enjoyed making them at home and taking them with me to our rituals.

Preparation meant frequent journeys up and down four flights of stairs from the basement kitchen to the attic room. I placed the cakes and wine on a tray to take them up to the temple, but I was not permitted to leave the tray outside the room for use after the ritual. It had to be replaced in the basement kitchen and collected again after the ritual was over, which meant an extra two journeys to and from the kitchen. The altar accoutrements were laid out in specific positions corresponding with the element they represented. For example, an accoutrement related to the water element would be placed on the left of the altar in the westerly direction.

The men would light the candles and incense while Beatrice bathed and prepared herself to appear before us. We stood quietly in line to await Beatrice, but Paul and Perry would giggle at times like naughty schoolboys! She entered the temple with her hair still wet from bathing as she examined each of us from head to foot. I could see by her expression how proud she was of her coven. The Alexandrian rituals were more serious than the Gardnerian ones we experienced, but this was also a constant reminder of the seriousness of our commitment.

On one occasion, while awaiting Beatrice's appearance, Robert entered the temple and instructed me to remove a pentacle ring from my right index finger. I frequently wore many rings and usually removed them before a ritual, but on this occasion, I was distracted by the preparations and had forgotten.

During the following coven meeting, Robert spoke about members who attempt to elevate themselves to second degree before they are ready. Beatrice was not present for this part of the meeting, and I sensed he alluded to the ring I forgot to remove when I entered the temple. He gave the impression this had been intentional. However, I was fully aware it would take much more than the mere wearing of a ring to attain a second degree. I did not challenge him on this matter and let it pass.

Robert also spoke about invoking elementals, saying they should be asked to enter the sacred space and never summoned. I recalled Sally invoking the elementals with strength and passion, so I followed her example, and once again it seemed Robert's remark was directed at me. This caused me to question the words written in our Book of Shadows for invocation of elementals: "I summon, stir, and call ye forth." It made no sense to me, but I didn't feel that I could discuss it with them.

Beatrice and Robert asked us to research our own birth charts and take notes on their symbols and meanings. They were curious to know which aspects of our charts that we agreed or disagreed with. We were shown examples of birth charts on their computer, when Paul noticed a list of stored charts that belonged to their friends and acquaintances. He assumed this knowledge could be used as a tool for manipulation.

When studying my own chart, I thought its interpretation of my personality was not totally accurate. It stated I would give total devotion and loyalty to people or projects that I was passionate about, and this information would have been a favourable aspect for recruiting me into their group. However, the effect of being raised within a religious 'cult' in my formative years meant I had the ability to sever emotional ties and contact with family or close friends, as I was accustomed to doing this with those who left my parents' religion. I retained this ability to sever ties from anyone if necessary, as some childhood teachings are ingrained, but this aspect would not be included in my chart.

Our coven worked with each of the four elements over a period of six weeks.

We used meditation, and during the final weeks, we created a ritual for that element. Each one brought something to the surface: water brought emotional situations, fire brought anger issues, air brought communication problems, and earth raised stability and security issues within the home. Paul disliked the repercussions of each exercise, but we managed to resolve the issues that arose.

At a coven meeting, Beatrice and Robert announced that they had volunteered our group to perform a play for the open Autumn Equinox ritual in London. They decided to act out the legend of Ishtar and Ereshkigal. Robert would be the narrator, and the rest of us would play a character with minimal dialogue. I would play Ishtar, Queen of the Heavens. We sat at their dining room table and they read us their script.

Ishtar descends to the Underworld to meet with her sister, Ereshkigal (Beatrice had chosen to play this role). The Gatekeeper (played by Perry) opened each gate for Ishtar to enter, but as she passed through, he would remove some of her jewellery and clothes symbolising her power. (Beatrice suggested that the Gatekeeper performed this in a forceful way to create an intense energy of "rape.") When all of Ishtar's power had been taken from her, she would then be at the mercy of Ereshkigal, who hung her sister on a hook to rot. Dumuzi (the character chosen for Paul) descended to the Underworld to rescue Ishtar, but Ereshkigal was strongly attracted to him and offered Dumuzi anything he wished. He requested a drink from the water skin that hung on the hook (Ishtar's rotting body). The Gatekeeper then sprinkled waters of life upon her and Ishtar was revived. Ereshkigal allowed Ishtar to leave, but insisted that Dumuzi stay with her, so he sacrificed himself for Ishtar's freedom.

I was a little disturbed by this story, and later discovered that the actual story is quite different from the version they created. I have also discovered there are many versions, but I chose to compare this with the oldest Sumerian version.[1]

The characters that were left out of the 'ritual play,' but played a significant part in the Sumerian version, were Inanna's (Ishtar's) handmaiden Ninsubur, the Galla, two genderless creatures, and the father-God Enki.

In our performance, Ishtar was presented as a "damsel in distress" and Erishkigal as the powerful sibling. Ishtar gladly gave up her adornments and clothes, but there was no force or "energy of rape." Beatrice preferred to play a powerful character with no physical weaknesses. Dumuzi was the 'knight in shining armour' who came

1     https://www.worldhistory.org/article/215/inannas-descent-a-sumerian-tale-of-injustice/

to the underworld to save Ishtar. He asked for the waters of life, and sprinkled them upon her. Erishkigal was strongly attracted to Dumuzi, and he had to agree to stay in the underworld with her so that she would let Ishtar go. Although Ishtar had her freedom and regained her power, Erishkigal had power over Ishtar's husband and took him from her.

Our costumes for setting up the sacred space were full white face masks and black hooded cloaks. While we were discussing them, Robert mentioned that Alex Sanders was well known for his use of masks within ritual. He felt that because we were an Alexandrian coven, we should do the same.

The character of Ishtar required three face masks and two costumes. I created one of the costumes myself: a white cotton dress with Velcro sewn at the seams (as it had to be torn from my body) and a sky-blue cloak decorated with silver stars. I purchased a flesh-coloured body suit from a dance retail outlet, as well as a mask that would be painted to resemble a corpse. I needed many items of jewellery that I would remove when passing through each of the gates. Costumes for the role of Ishtar required the most work, but Robert assisted with the painting of masks, and an artist who was a friend of Galadriel volunteered to paint the bodysuit.

I expressed my concerns to Paul about this performance, particularly the "energy of rape" that had been mentioned, but he thought I had been given the starring role and felt it would be good for my development. It amused him how Ereshkigal's character suited Beatrice in many ways.

Paul often played the role of "naughty little boy" within the coven, but the more he misbehaved, the harder Beatrice made him work. Learning the words was difficult for him, especially with the lengthy Alexandrian rituals. Whenever he attempted to recite an invocation, he would tremble and perspiration would drip from his face. Paul seemed to handle other stressful aspects of life quite well and took matters in his stride, so I was unaccustomed to seeing him react this way.

Paul was also of the opinion that Beatrice enjoyed wielding power over him, because of the high rank he held within his occupation. I had noticed this during his initiation. During one of our full moon rituals, Beatrice told Paul to set up the entire sacred space by himself, though he was permitted to delegate tasks to the other members if needed. Paul would not give Beatrice the satisfaction of asking for help and was determined to accomplish it all himself. When the time for our ritual arrived, I hoped he would be successful, and he accomplished the task well. Paul may not have thought this fair at the time, but by setting him this task, Beatrice used his stubbornness to help him overcome his difficulties.

I recall a time when Beatrice baked a Beltane cake where one of the slices would be marked with a black spot caused by food colouring. Whoever picked the slice with the spot would be scourged and have to give up something as a kind of sacrifice for the year, similar to lent. Paul boasted for weeks that he would not choose the piece of cake with a black spot. When the time came for us to choose a slice, I noticed that Beatrice had cut one piece larger than the rest. She turned the plate so it was nearest to him, but he did not choose it, thus avoiding the slice with the black spot. He was triumphant. Perry, bless him, was the one who chose that particular slice.

– Dancing with the Morris team in Devon

– The sword used in my Alexndrian initiation given to me by my Priestess. Photo John Isaac

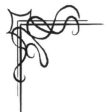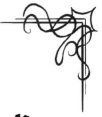

# Chapter 11
## Events & Misunderstanding

*September 2002*

After the closure of our psychic physical phenomena group, I cleared the room and created a small temple for meditation and magical work. I painted the walls Egyptian blue, and the skirting boards and shelves gold. I also purchased a stencil of Egyptian figures and painted a row of them on the uppermost part of the walls using the remaining gold paint. Beatrice had mentioned that her priestess, Galadriel, had life-size painted illustrations on her temple walls of Egyptian deities. This provided inspiration for decorating my room. A blue rug filled the floor space, and a long, dark, mahogany sideboard I had previously used in the lounge with the Gardnerian group was transferred to this room, as it was an ideal surface for an altar with a storage cupboard for accoutrements. My statue of Sekhmet stood proudly upon the altar alongside other statues of Isis and Anubis, and my working tools. The temple, though small, had a peaceful ambiance, and I used it frequently for personal rituals and meditations.

I was extremely careful about who I left Ruben with, so Paul and I could not always get a babysitter for our coven meetings. Paul suggested I attend alone and he would stay with Ruben. This occurred frequently, and on one occasion, Beatrice contacted me by telephone and requested Paul's presence at their next ritual, instructing me to stay at home with Ruben on this occasion. It was also Paul's birthday, which meant we would be apart that evening. I enjoyed the rituals and was disappointed I had to remain at home. It was late when Paul arrived home that evening, and although he enjoyed the attention he received from the group on his birthday, he commented he was unimpressed by the shamanic trance drumming that took place in their garden. When I attended our next Morris practice, I greeted Beatrice and she smirked at me, knowing I was disappointed about staying at home, missing the ritual, and being apart from Paul on his birthday.

I recall a time when our coven met and agreed to cast a spell to save local woodland from being obliterated. We raised energy for the spell, standing in a circle while holding a cord between us, and took small steps to the right and left, creating a rocking motion. As we did this and the energy heightened, I remember groaning ecstatically as the energy became more intense. This affected the other group members and I heard a small whimper from one of the men. When we had built sufficient energy, there were beads of sweat on our foreheads, and I recall Beatrice and Robert exchanging glances. We then sat down to meditate with the energy raised, and all of us visualised a bird hovering in the centre of the circle that flew away. The following week, Robert showed us an article in the local newspaper that reported the woodland would not be interfered with, as they discovered a rare species of bird living there!

Our coven members planned to attend the 2002 Summer Solstice event at Stonehenge, and it was the first time we had experienced this. The group travelled separately and arranged to meet at the venue. Ruben was extremely excited about the overnight celebrations and staying up until sunrise. Parking of vehicles was allocated in a nearby field, and we spent some time studying the variety of transport there. Large removal vans were converted into rooms with carpets and curtains, and one of them had a crystal chandelier hanging inside. As we walked towards the site, we noticed policemen were patrolling the area, and one of them was engaged in an aggressive conversation with a Pagan man. This was the only confrontation I witnessed at the event. Many people were delighted to be at the ancient site, particularly as the fences were removed around the stones. As we neared the stones, I received a mobile phone text message from Beatrice informing us they were lying upon the grass at the right-hand side of the stone circle. Ruben pointed at a reclining couple thinking it may be them. However, the activity they were engaged in confirmed otherwise, and I hastily moved him on!

We eventually found Beatrice, Robert, and Perry, and we all sat together observing the celebrations going on around us. A gathering of many drummers created a wonderful rhythm that encouraged dancing, and one of them winked at me. I marvelled at the sight of a man dressed in long robes, leading a crowd of revellers around the stones, holding a horned staff ablaze with fire. The celebrations invoked strong ancient energies that transported us back in time to rituals of the Old Ways. Unfortunately, the bright green spot lights illuminating the stones with an eerie glow, were a reminder of the modern times we live in. A large duvet was spread out on the grass in front of us covering six moving bodies, and occasionally, a head would appear for a breath of air, before disappearing under it again. If I had prior knowledge of the adult activities at this event, I would not have brought Ruben.

After a while, I decided to walk amongst the stones to connect with their energies. When I emerged from them, I assumed that I had come out from the same direction I entered, but could not see anything familiar. I wandered around for a while until Perry noticed me and escorted me back to the group. On reflection, I had been what the Cornish describe as "piskie led."

Just before the sun rose, people nearby shouted to the policemen to turn off their green lights, and we stood facing the east in silence. The crowd began to cheer at the time of sunrise, but unfortunately, the clouds had obstructed our view of it. It was a memorable experience, but not one I wish to repeat, as some individuals there had sadly shown no respect for the stones or the site.

We attended a folk festival in Whitby with our Morris team, and I saw a man there that I had met previously at one of our local festivals. I remember that as we walked to the next dance area, we passed him in the street wearing the same kit as our male members. The teenage members from our team greeted Ron with a hug and introduced him to me. Ron seemed a friendly, happy, affectionate man, but when I caught up with Beatrice, who did not stop to greet him, she informed me they no longer communicated with Ron, because he once referred to Robert as "power crazy." I later discovered Ron was not only a former member of our Morris team, but also of our coven. Some team members remained in contact with him despite the fallout, and I heard from Beatrice and Robert that Ron and his wife suddenly moved away after a disagreement. They had not informed anyone of their departure and went on to create their own Morris team in Whitby. They came face to face with Robert and Beatrice in a shop selling gothic attire, and apparently, they 'froze' for a minute or two, then made a hasty retreat. I wondered what had occurred to make them leave the coven and Morris team so abruptly and move far away, but it was obviously a raw subject that I did not want to raise with them.

Our coven members were busy preparing costumes for the 2002 Autumn Equinox ritual, and I was instructed by Beatrice to visit the home of Galadriel, their priestess, to wear the bodysuit while it was painted for the "corpse scene." They gave me her address and vague directions to the property. Unfamiliar with the area,

I found the directions rather confusing. After searching for a while, I contacted Galadriel by mobile phone, who awaited my arrival with her male friend. I had difficulty understanding their directions, as they were constantly laughing and sounded as though they were intoxicated. The phone signal was also erratic, so I continued my search and asked members of the public who passed by, but no one recognized the address. After three hours of searching, I had to return home and collect Ruben from school. I sent Beatrice a mobile phone text to let her know I was unable to find the address and of my return home.

Beatrice, who was extremely angry, contacted us by telephone that evening. Paul answered her call and she demanded to speak to me, but when he warned me of her current mood, I refused to take the call until she had calmed down. Beatrice threatened dismissal from the coven if I did not immediately speak to her. Paul attempted to calm the situation by reasoning with her, and he succeeded. I suspected Galadriel had reacted angrily when I did not arrive, and directed this at Beatrice, as it was her initiate that failed to attend. Beatrice left a message with Paul demanding I contact Galadriel immediately to apologise, and I did so the following day, allowing time for heightened emotions to settle.

Galadriel was cool and calm as she explained that due to my absence, she had to wear the bodysuit while her friend painted it. The paint soaked through the bodysuit and ruined a new item of expensive white lingerie she wore underneath. I offered to replace it, and she described it as a small white lace item that cost eight pounds from a highly-priced retail outlet. I explained the difficulty I had in finding her place of residence and offered to transport her to our final rehearsal so that we would know where to find her for any future visits. Galadriel refused my offer and replied I would never have reason to visit her home again, so would not need to know its location. The conversation ended there. I immediately travelled into the town to purchase Galadriel's item of lingerie, and on my return, I found a message on our answering machine from Robert. He attempted to inject some humour into the situation by commenting that he had wanted to speak to me, but I must be in town purchasing underwear. This confirmed that Galadriel had contacted them with an update on our conversation.

A few days later, Paul and I arrived at the venue for Morris' practice for our final ritual rehearsal. We knew Galadriel would be there with Beatrice and Robert. Paul commented that we would not stay for the rehearsal if the atmosphere continued to be hostile. When we entered the practice hall, Perry greeted us, unaware of recent events. I immediately approached Galadriel to give her the new lingerie and once again apologised. I also reimbursed Robert with money for the petrol he used when he apparently searched for me on his motorcycle. I apologised to them both, and as I walked away, Beatrice followed me and gave me a tearful hug. This surprised me, as I believed Paul's opinion about her lacking in emotion. The show of affection helped settle the situation. Robert once alluded to the difficult time they had while training in Galadriel's coven, and there were times Beatrice wanted to leave. I believed this after experiencing her reaction. Although this incident seemed to be resolved, Paul decided he no longer wished to continue as a member of the coven, and informed me that he would leave after the Autumn Equinox ritual.

During our rehearsals, Paul annoyed Beatrice when he performed the only line he had in the ritual. He told his friends that they deliberately gave him only one line so that he didn't mess it up. When he acted the role of Dumuzi and asked for a drink from the water skin, he did so in a commanding tone rather than a request. Beatrice instructed him to request the water skin in a respectful manner rather than saying "Hey, you, give me the water skin so I may drink from it!" Paul had related this to friends of ours, announcing that he would do as she asked during rehearsals, but on the night of the performance he will do it his way. Some of our friends planned to attend the ritual mainly to witness this.

We arrived in London for our Autumn Equinox ritual performance, and during the preparations, Beatrice and Robert asked on more than one occasion if all was well. Paul leaving the coven had been on my mind, and they seemed to sense I was preoccupied. When we were ready and the audience arrived, we entered the darkened room in our white face masks and black cloaks to set up the sacred space while the loud dramatic rock music played. We were instructed that every move needed to be exaggerated, so when I blessed the salt and water with a huge athame, I held it high above my head with both hands before it slowly descended into the receptacles. Robert choreographed our movements so that when we walked away from the altar, instead of turning to the left to walk away, we turned to the right and formed a small circle before leaving, so that our cloaks created a wonderful swirl outwards with dramatic effect. After the sacred space was prepared, I left the performance area to change.

We began to perform "The Descent of Ishtar." As Robert narrated the story, I passed through each gate as her jewellery, crown, and clothes were gradually removed by Perry while I struggled and protested. Acting this part of the story was

93

not as bad as I thought it would be, as I felt great affection for Perry, so the energy did not feel aggressive. When I had passed through all the gates and Ishtar lost her power, Beatrice as Ereshkigal approached me to gloat, placing her hand under my chin, lifting my head to look into my eyes before aggressively pushing my head away. This action was far from gentle. During rehearsals, and even at the performance, I closed my eyes during this part, as I refused to see the enjoyment in Beatrice's eyes. I was then stripped of Ishtar's white robe, revealing the corpse body suit, and placed upon a small block in front of a pole, giving the impression of a body hanging on a hook.

Perry, as the Gatekeeper, changed my glamorous mask for the corpse mask while a strobe light flashed, and the volume of rock music increased. There was a stunned silence from the audience at this point. Paul kept his word when playing the role of Dumuzi and spoke the line in his way. However, Beatrice was so deeply involved in her role as Ereshkigal by then that she did not seem to notice. Ishtar was then brought back to life, Paul replaced my glamorous mask, and I quickly escaped through all gates while replacing the robes, jewellery, and crown. This was quite a task, as it all had to be done in haste. I then stood proudly in front of the audience, robed and powerful once again. Beatrice had Paul on his knees, forcing him to drink potions, rendering him helpless. When the play had ended, we returned to our black cloaks and white face masks to hand out libations to the audience. I noticed when I approached someone to speak to them, they would not look at me while I wore the mask, as it made them uncomfortable.

After the ritual, we received mixed feedback from the audience, as this version of the story was particularly dark. Most open rituals at the venue were light-hearted and joyous celebrations. Galadriel had been drinking wine while awaiting our return backstage in the dressing room. She spoke and acted surprisingly differently when intoxicated. Our group were all delighted with the performance, joining hands and literally jumping with happiness. We celebrated its success. Paul was upset, while I felt uncomfortable and emotionally exhausted, as we had been through a tough time during the preparation for this ritual. I was also aware that Paul's decision to leave the coven would cause more difficulties in the days ahead.

Paul told me that Robert had stated that all of our coven members had officers' roles within the Morris team, and therefore the coven had power over it. This was something we had not thought about. It was often a source of amusement that three of the officers were in occupations that involved law enforcement. When Paul took on the role of Squire for the male Morris team, he did not realise it would include pressurising male dancers to wear the correct kit. Paul received instructions from Beatrice to inform male dancers that they would not be permitted to perform at events if they arrived without their full kit. One dancer had deliberately flouted the team rules because he disliked Beatrice, and this infuriated her. I recall Beatrice and Robert standing behind Paul, looking over his shoulder, as he informed this member if he arrived at an event without his full kit, he would not be permitted to dance. Paul became less popular with team members, and this created additional problems. He then announced his resignation from the role of Squire at the next annual general meeting. When he read out the reason for his resignation, the male dancers conversed amongst themselves instead of listening to him. I noticed Paul's voice gradually decreased in volume to almost a whisper as he finished reading his reasons for resignation. The officers then went on to discuss other business, and when Paul gave his opinion on a particular matter, Beatrice harshly replied they were no longer interested in his opinions, because he had resigned as an officer. Paul lowered his head and said no more.

Within my roles as Foreman and Squire, I had no problems with female dancers wearing incorrect kits, as they loved their attire; they were graceful, beautiful, and they looked fabulous. I recall one man who approached us after one of our performances, and he described us in his deep husky voice as "dark, gothic, and sexy!" One of our dancers asked him to repeat this, and we all laughed at this request. I did, however, have other difficulties with a few over-sensitive personalities in the women's team.

The Morris team attended a performance one Sunday afternoon in the summer outside a beautiful country inn. I chose two sets of four female dancers for our next performance, and after explaining their positions, Beatrice stated I had placed the dancers in the wrong places. I knew her assumption was incorrect, as I had been teaching them throughout the practice season and knew their positions well. Beatrice still insisted she was right. I followed her to the performance area and stood back while she directed the dancers to the positions she thought were correct. As the music began, one of the dancers approached her and explained she had been placed in the wrong position. This meant the musicians had to stop and wait while the dancers rearranged themselves. This amused the audience. I glanced over at Beatrice, who stared defiantly back at me, and when we began our dance, my 'stick-clashing' was particularly aggressive. After the performance, she did not apologise, and no more was said on the matter. I did not understand why this had occurred. However, I had noticed frequent overriding of officer's decisions by Beatrice and Robert. I do acknowledge, however, that it is to their credit that our Morris team performed to such a high standard with the strict discipline and exact teaching they provided.

Paul and I discussed the coven and he still intended to leave, but said that if we wanted to stay in the Morris team, I had to remain in the coven. He arranged to visit Beatrice and Robert alone to tell them his decision and was with them for a period of three hours. Paul returned home triumphant, telling me he explained his reason for leaving the coven. He also flattered, hugged, and expressed his love for them, so as not to rouse their anger. They attempted to persuade him to remain, and expressed that even if he did leave, they would still continue to treat him as an initiate. Robert also warned him that my continuing development without him would change me in ways that could affect our relationship. Paul did not take the warning seriously, and was pleased the visit went according to his plan.

I arranged another appointment to see Alice the spirit medium for a consultation, and she informed me that Kevin, my father-in-law, had inquired about his watch. I was aware Paul had lost it, and although she made suggestions as to its whereabouts, we could not find it. Alice gave me guidance concerning my spiritual development, and advised that I should choose between development in the Craft or mediumship, as spreading myself between both would mean I would not excel at either. She invited me to her psychic development circle, and I considered this an honour, as she had such a good reputation.

I attended one evening, and discovered that six of the eight female members were smokers, which they did so continuously throughout the evening. I thought this showed little respect for Spirit or the important work we were doing. Alice also discussed "cold reading" by observation of a clients' facial expressions and actions. She also mentioned generational similarities when bringing through messages from spirit loved ones, stating that it isn't difficult to describe a client's grandparents, who will likely have the same characteristics as the client. Alice explained that these methods are a good way of "filling in" if you are not receiving messages from Spirit during a reading. This surprised me. However, I knew Alice was a genuine medium, as I had received specific evidence from her that she could not have obtained through only a cold reading.

I continued to attend coven meetings and rituals without Paul, and worked hard at completing all tasks required, particularly as there was one less member to assist with preparations. I set up the temple with Perry and Robert, and added extra energy into our magical work to compensate for Paul's absence. After our rituals and each meeting, I put away all accoutrements in their correct places. After we had feasted, Perry and I washed and dried the eating utensils, pots, and pans. Beatrice sat in her large antique 'throne' chair, directing us to places for putting away all utensils in cupboards and upon the shelves. This was our usual routine at each meeting, and by the time we completed our tasks, it was well past midnight. I had a twenty-two-mile journey home and needed to be up at seven the next morning to take Ruben to school. Perry lived only two streets away and did not have so far to go. On one occasion, I was tired and told them I needed to leave. However, Beatrice ignored my request and continued to drink her wine, which I took as a sign that we were not permitted to leave until she had finished.

When I attended the coven's Yuletide ritual, it was my intention to tell them I had decided to leave the coven. Beatrice, Robert, and I were born in the same year and close in age, but they treated me in the same way as my religious parents, and had the same level of fanaticism about their beliefs. I acknowledge that teaching someone correctly can be rather regimented at times. However, it was beginning to encroach on my personal life, too. That evening, no matter how I tried, the words I needed to say about leaving the coven would not come out. I found them too unapproachable, particularly after the incident at Autumn Equinox. I asked to leave early that evening, after the ritual ended, as this difficult situation had caused me to feel unwell.

After some deep discussion with Paul, we decided it would be easier to send Beatrice and Robert two letters, one for my resignation of membership from the coven, and the other for our resignation from the Morris team. We had enjoyed the majority of our time with them, but were aware of the serious repercussions that would likely occur if we remained in the Morris team after leaving the coven. We were aware their former coven members had left the Morris team, as they found the atmosphere too uncomfortable. I had already experienced a little of this when I resigned from my position as dance teacher for the female team, as Beatrice had to take over teaching again and worked me much harder than before. I recall her smirking at me when I stood there gasping for breath and dripping in perspiration after insisting we repeated a dance over and over until the new members got it right. We received an immediate reply the following day by letter from Beatrice and Robert, stating that there would be no more contact between us. They also requested our handwritten copies of the coven Book of Shadows. I had not heard of this before, so I sought advice from Pagan friends who were also members of a coven. They confirmed Beatrice and Robert had no right to ask for them. We heard that Beatrice informed members of her Morris team that I sent her a letter identical to the one we had supposedly sent to Sally when we left her Gardnerian group. This was untrue, as I conversed with Sally by telephone about leaving her group, and our reasons for departure were altogether different. When the vow of 'perfect love and perfect trust' is uttered within a coven situation, trust can only be obtained if you are confident your teachers are truthful with you and about you.

I have heard other Alexandrian initiates discuss their time in covens recently on social media groups, and it seemed they were all subjected to a high level of discipline and agreed with this method of teaching. They stated, 'nothing of value should be easily attained.' When I reflect on my time within the coven, I was not ready within my development to take that amount of discipline, and it was unfortunate this opportunity had not occurred when I had more experience and understanding. I have also researched 'cultish' behaviour within groups, and am now able to recognize the ones to avoid.

After leaving the coven, I avoided all magical groups and spent time away from the Pagan scene. I packed away all my Egyptian artefacts and gave them to Lorna to add to her Egyptian collection. This was a temporary measure to give me time for contemplation. I worked as a holistic therapist in her beauty salon, but we no longer worked together magically, as Lorna planned to emigrate to Australia with her family to live in the same country as her brother.

After a while, I returned to solitary magical practice, and Beatrice and Robert kept their word, severing all ties with us in the same way my parents shunned me when I left their religion. I missed Morris dancing, but it was time to move on and discover new activities. No one, however, can take away my positive memories, particularly the auspicious day I observed twelve female dancers, who gave an excellent performance because of my teaching. I received unexpected praise from Beatrice and Robert after the event. I cannot fault their excellent teaching structure, and I have learnt some valuable skills that I still use from the time I spent with them.

– The altar in my small temple.

– Dancing with the Morris team in Whitby.

# Chapter 12
## Moving On

*February 2003 – March 2003*

Ruben passed his eleven-plus examination at school and was placed on a waiting list for a place at our preferred grammar school. This was a matter of concern, as it was the only school that would accept him. During the selection process, parents need to state a first and second choice, but schools that are not your first choice can be a little awkward. Our second-choice of school would only offer Ruben a place if he did not pass his examination, so all hopes were on the grammar school. The waiting list would not move for another two months when all test results were completed, which left us in a form of 'limbo.'

About a month later near Imbolc, Paul awoke suddenly at three in the morning on hearing a knocking sound, and thought someone may be at the front door or window. On investigation, he found nothing. At six that same morning, we suddenly awoke to the sound of our television at high volume. When Paul returned to investigate, the remote controls were where we had left them the night before, and Ruben was asleep in his bedroom. There was no physical explanation for this occurrence. At ten that morning, I received a telephone call from the grammar school secretary, informing us that the waiting list had moved earlier than expected and Ruben had his place. I sensed the spirit of Kevin, my father-in-law, may have attempted to alert us that something would happen that day. He had always shown a keen interest in Ruben's education. Ruben had apparently seen his grandfather in spirit a few weeks after his death while all three of us were having a 'lie-in' together one Sunday morning. Ruben told us he stood at the end of our bed, watching us and smiling. He is comfortable with the spirit world, so this vision did not disturb or frighten him.

I purchased a book entitled Channelling: What It Is and How To Do It by Lita De Alverdi. It explains in detail the developmental stages of spirit mediumship, and I used it as a reference book for members of my own psychic development circle. We achieved some good results from their development at this time by using guided meditations for connection with the spirit.

We were visited by Leonard and Louise, the couple we met at the Egyptian Group. We walked to the local woodland together and explored the nearby ruins of the eleventh century church. Leonard updated us with news of a new friendship he had with Rockbone, who were a rock band, as well as a coven. They were interested in networking with Leonard because of his American origin and his contacts there. The band had also been searching for a property in the United States. Louise had supported all his ventures, and therefore agreed to sell their home so that he could donate his half of the proceeds to the commune. Leonard moved to France with Rockbone, but as an older man who enjoyed his home comforts, I could not see this new way of life being successful, as the band members were younger and used to moving from place to place. We heard that the group had thirteen coven members: ten bisexual women and three men. They did not care where they stayed and led a seriously promiscuous life, displaying this on stage during their performances, as well as off stage in their everyday lives. I asked Louise if she was concerned about Leonard associating with them, and she replied his personal life has nothing to do with her. Two months after he moved out and they sold their home, Leonard returned from France, exhausted, thinner, and without money or transport. Paul helped him by providing an old car for transport. Louise was understandably upset, as they had sold their property. However, she kindly allowed Leonard to move into her tiny apartment. It upset me knowing they were taken advantage of, as I knew only too well how attractive some groups can appear. The harsh reality only surfaces when a person is deeply involved.

I attended Reiki 'shares' at the home of Ernie and Shirley, the couple I met at the Scole Seminar in Norfolk. 'Shares' are arranged for Reiki practitioners to treat one another. The wonderful experience of lying upon a couch encased in strong healing energy from nine pairs of hands is exceptionally powerful. A concentrated ten-minute treatment is all a person needs, as all areas of the body are receiving energy at the same time. I met Tessa there, who was a holistic therapist like myself. She recommended a local Yoga teacher and invited me to his classes. I attended them for a few months, and he taught advanced postures, chanting, and meditation. I was impressed by this, and he seemed like a wonderful, spiritual man. Paul refused to believe he was genuine, and stated that many men use these opportunities to attract impressionable women. Members of his classes were pleased with his teaching and considered him a highly spiritual person, until they visited a summer Yoga retreat he had organised in France. His claims of abstaining from alcohol and being celibate were proven false when certain unprofessional activities took place. This resulted in many members leaving his classes, and Paul was triumphant that yet again he was right. I took Paul to see the psychic medium Colin Fry at a venue that was full of women. He said a man could 'take his pick' there as so many women would love to have a spiritual partner. One of them even asked Paul for his phone number!

A member of our former Morris team told us that Beatrice and Robert had decided to leave the team at the end of the year. This surprised me, as I knew how difficult they found releasing any control to others. They were also the founder members and had dedicated seven years of their lives to teaching and performing. I remembered that they had grown weary of the constant organising and teaching while we were there, so making this decision would also relieve them of the responsibility. Perry was still in their coven, and when the team suggested that we may return after Robert and Beatrice's departure, one member told me that Perry allegedly said he would leave the Morris team if we did so.

In March 2003, we attended the Devon and Cornwall Pagan seminar at the Camelot Castle Hotel in Tintagel. I had longed to experience this event since I first heard about it, and was delighted the 'powers that be' gave us this opportunity. It would also provide the opportunity to network with other Pagans leading up to our move to Cornwall. Camelot Castle Hotel is a grand venue, and at this time, its interior had a mediaeval theme with burgundy painted walls, embroidered upholstery on the chairs, and heavy velvet drapes with large tassels hanging from huge windows. As we made our way across the tiled floors to the grand staircase, we passed a large highly polished circular table with ornate chairs surrounding it. We stayed in one of the large rooms and found they were quite basic compared to the ambience of the ground floor. There were standard double and single beds, and a small cabinet that contained a shower and lavatory. Ruben enjoyed standing on a stone balcony outside the bedroom window, looking down on the cliffs and out to sea. We noticed a large labyrinth maze imprinted on the land below us, so we walked the maze, which Ruben enjoyed.

The organisers of the Conference were aware that we had Ruben with us and gave prior warning of a talk containing adult content during one part of the programme. It was suggested that we take him elsewhere during this talk, and Paul volunteered to take him for a stroll around the grounds. The subject of the talk was the work of Aleister Crowley, his rituals, the Great Rite, and ingredients of the ceremonial cakes containing semen and menstrual blood. I wondered how many coven members knew of the ingredients, as this may have affected their enjoyment of eating them. During the lunch break, I browsed the stalls and met the charming professor who was one of the speakers that day. He recognized me from the London conference and explained that he was searching the stalls for a sickle. I paused at another stall in the entrance hall selling Gothic attire. It was then that I heard someone call out to Patrick, the stall holder, who is also a renowned artist. I turned to see who spoke, and saw a small confident woman striding into the grand entrance hall wearing a soft crooked hat, a white t-shirt, jeans, and a black waistcoat. I later discovered her name was Alexandra and that she was one of the organisers. She greeted me with a "Hellooo!!" in a cheeky but charming manner that came across as rather flirtatious. As she neared the entrance, she continued to walk backwards still smiling at me, then she disappeared through the heavy wooden rotating doors. There was something unique about Alexandra in her appearance and energy that made such an impression on me. She remained in my thoughts for the rest of the day. The conference ended with a closing ritual performed by a Nordic magical group. I was intrigued by this path and their ritual, as my paternal side is of Scandinavian descent.

Carolyn Hillier and Nigel Shaw performed their breath-taking music and songs during the evening. It was the first time I had seen them, and their powerful soul connection was evident as they performed together. I recognized her voice as the woman who sang to the beat of a drum when I visited the home of Suzie, my first pagan contact. I sat upon a chair in the front row, listening to a haunting tune composed by Nigel entitled "The Waterfall," and gazed out of the window at the sea as this music filled the room. During this emotional moment, I glanced behind me and saw Alexandra standing at the back of the room with her back against the wall while conversing with someone. I did not realise how significant meeting her would be in years to come. I thoroughly enjoyed the seminar, as it was rather small and intimate compared to Pagan events in London. There was a warm and friendly atmosphere, too, and I had just begun conversing with a group of women when Paul told me it was time to leave. I agreed to go, but wished I had stayed longer.

– Camelot Castle Hotel and the ground's maze

– The entrance of the hotel with the rotary doors that Alexandra exited from after first meeting

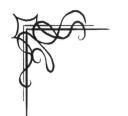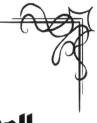

# Chapter 13
## Networking in Cornwall

*May 2003 – September 2004*

During 2002 and 2003, I experienced two family bereavements. The first one was the death of my paternal uncle, and the second my brother. I was unaware of my uncle's passing until I heard the sad news from close friends of mine, so I contacted the undertakers, who informed me his funeral occurred a week ago. I visited the cemetery alone with a bouquet of flowers, and with the assistance of a man who worked there, I eventually found his grave. Fortunately, I met my uncle by chance two months before his death, as I was working in the area where he lived. I noticed him walking along the street and we conversed for a while. He asked for a hug, then continued his walk with a happy smile. I sent a letter to my parents, expressing how upset I was that they had not informed me about my uncle's passing, as we had no contact due to religious shunning of those who leave the sect.

During the Easter weekend of 2003, on what is known as Good Friday, my father contacted me by telephone to inform me of my brother's sudden passing. I attended his funeral in my parents' local cemetery chapel, as they could not have the service in their church as my brother had not been raised within the religion. He had lived in a residential hospital since childhood because of his severe autism. Regardless, my parents still requested one of their religious funeral services, and the Elders obliged. I refused to enter the chapel for the service, as Paul stated that I did not need to hear this 'rubbish' again. We waited by the graveside, though, which provided me the opportunity to sit with my brother's coffin until the burial, as my mother did not want it in the chapel. I had not been invited to the wake, as many members of my parents' religion were there to support them, even though the majority had not met him. I was unsure whether the 'shunning rule' would still be enforced on this occasion, so I returned home and performed a personal last rites Requiem for him within my small temple. My brother was ten years my senior, but he was still quite young when he passed. I have vivid memories of the many times we visited him that will always remain with me.

The Lammas edition of the Pagan Dawn magazine contained an article and photographs of the Eastbourne Folk Festival, along with our performance with the Morris team. While browsing its pages, I also noticed an advertisement for new members to join a 'Craft of the Cornish' group. Experiences from working with magical groups in Kent had deterred me from working with another, but as this was a Cornish Craft group, I sensed this opportunity would not often arise. From its description, the work would be deeply rooted within Cornish magic, and I had yearned for an opportunity to learn more about the Old Craft of Cornwall. I sent an email to the address provided, expressing an interest in joining their group, and explained our plans to move to Cornwall. I suggested we could use the six years leading up to our move to become better acquainted via email correspondence and yearly visits before they made their decision. I included sufficient information about my life and magical experience, then eagerly awaited a reply.

Paul, Ruben, and I visited our local folk festival in May 2003, and met with some members of our former Morris team. They were pleased to see us, and this meeting provided an opportunity to explain to them our reasons for leaving. Beatrice had attended a Yoga event that day, so was absent from the festival. However, while we were with the Morris team in the hotel bar, Robert arrived with Perry. They engaged in a private conversation, then Robert left the hotel and Perry joined us at the table. It was good to see them again. Perry was friendly, but a little reserved, as this once again placed him in an awkward position. I sensed he may have received instructions to check on our conversation with other team members. We enjoyed seeing them all, as it was their day off from performing, and this gave us an opportunity to spend more time with them.

I completed my Reiki Master/Teacher course in May 2003 and obtained a diploma. It was not my original plan to take my Reiki development to this level, but I had good results from using it, and it naturally became an important part of my spiritual journey and way of life. The two-day Master course was intense. However, Tarran, my Reiki Master, is a fabulous teacher. We learnt advanced meditations and how to provide Reiki attunements and empowerments to students, including new activation symbols and channelling different levels of energy. Before teaching one's own students, time is needed to digest all new information, and practice is required on various methods for teaching all three levels of Reiki. One ambition I had at this time was to set up a holistic retreat in Cornwall providing Reiki treatments, courses, and holistic therapies. I later discovered this ambition is a popular fantasy of many therapists who move here. In the past, I discussed this idea with Beatrice, who stated she would never move to Cornwall, as there would be too much competition between so many complementary therapists in a small area of the South West.

I heard that Ben and Jill at St. Nectan's waterfall organised an 'end of summer season' event on All Hallows Eve each year entitled "Lighting of a Thousand Candles." I yearned to experience this, so Paul and I decided to travel to Cornwall on Samhain 2003. We owned a fabulous Hyundai Coupe Mark 1 F2 sports car with a black exterior and black leather interior. I referred to the car as my 'bat-mobile,' and Paul purchased a black silhouette of a bat for the car's rear window as a birthday gift for me. It received a few amused expressions from Ruben's teachers when I collected him from school. During our journey to Cornwall, we stopped halfway through the journey at a petrol station on the A303. I entered the shop to use their inside public lavatory and discovered the door was locked. I waited for some time outside the cubicle and heard a rustling sound within, as if the person occupying it may have been reading a newspaper. After a while, the cubicle seemed quiet. Concerned about the welfare of the occupant, I knocked on the door to check all was well, and it opened to reveal an empty cubicle! After this incident, Ruben referred to it as the 'haunted loo' each year as we passed. Our journey to Cornwall on this occasion was the quickest I had experienced, taking three and a half hours to travel 265 miles in our sports car, instead of the usual seven hours.

We arrived at St. Nectan's waterfall by early evening. It was raining heavily. We gathered with other visitors in the meditation room, waiting for the rain to ease. Two women arrived who appeared to be around sixty years of age, wearing identical head scarves and raincoats. They had sharp pointed facial features, and I asked if they were twins, to which they replied that they were sisters, but not twins. They complimented me on my black velvet cloak, which suited the occasion. Ruben wore a small cloak and his wizard's hat. The rain eventually eased, and we slowly descended the steep slate steps leading to the bottom of the waterfall. The visitors were given ten tea light candles each to place within the cavities of the rock face near the waterfall. The ambiance of the falling water surrounded by flickering candles was a wonderful sight to behold. One hundred visitors were required to see a thousand candles at the site, but because of the wet weather, there were only twenty. Two hundred candles still created a wonderful ambiance.

As I neared the waterfall, I heard strong voices singing chants. I discovered it was the two sisters who had removed their scarves and raincoats, singing by their flickering candles next to the waterfall. This was surprising, as it is usually difficult to be heard above the tremendous force of the water. I recognised the chants from the Museum of Witchcraft soundtrack that constantly played during our visits. A while later, the sisters had disappeared. I asked the other visitors, including Ben, the owner, where they were, but no one had seen them leave. Intriguingly, there is a granite gravestone slab near the waterfall covering the grave where two sisters are buried. Could it be that on this Samhain night, the two sisters that sang so beautifully had returned for a while?

When it was time for us to leave, Paul had forgotten his torch and thought the glen too dangerous to walk through in the dark after heavy rainfall. Instead, we walked along the narrow lane behind the glen. It was well after midnight as we slowly made our way along the dark lane. Ruben, although excited, was a little apprehensive. About half way down the lane, I noticed a white misty figure standing on the left hand side of the lane. Paul described the same vision, so I knew my eyes were not deceiving me. I held on to the back of Paul's coat and Ruben held on to mine. We giggled like excited children on a 'ghost walk' until we eventually reached the car park. We began our journey and arrived home in the early hours of the morning. What a memorable and magical adventure that was!

Paul and I visited Cornwall for a week-long vacation in August of 2004, and we had beautiful summer weather. He had purchased a small video camera to capture footage of our journey through Boscastle, Tintagel, Rocky Valley, and St. Nectan's Waterfall. We were then able to view these videos at home, providing virtual visits to these places. Soon after our return from Cornwall, my psychic development circle met, and after a guided meditation, Irene, one of our members, sensed the presence of a Cornish water spirit that had apparently followed me home. One week after our visit to Cornwall, we heard Boscastle had been seriously flooded. We viewed distressing footage on a television news channel, seeing the village engulfed by sea water. Rescue helicopters lifted residents from buildings, and we noticed a car identical to our own carried out to sea from the car park. Our family and friends contacted us by telephone to ensure we were home safely from our vacation, as they were aware we regularly visited this village. Paul contacted the B.B.C information centre by telephone to confirm that Gary and his staff at the Museum were safe. He heard that the majority of telephone calls to the centre were inquiries about the Museum, and the following day, Gary gave a short television interview to journalists. He was understandably bewildered, explaining the awful state of the Museum and how long it would take for all residents to recover from the flood. He sadly lost a large collection of artefacts that were swept out to sea, but fortunately, the building remained intact. The beautiful stone bridge over the river had gone, and the Harbour Lights shop opposite the Museum was destroyed by the flood water. It was a devastating time for all the village residents. We also heard that the water in Rocky Valley and St. Nectan's waterfall rose by ten feet in height, and flooded the ground floor of Ben and Jill's cottage at the top of the waterfall. The tremendous unpredictable power of the sea spirits cannot be controlled, and what occurred that day seemed to instigate a time of thorough cleansing and change for the area.

I was delighted to receive a reply from a member of the Craft of the Cornish group. A young man named Tony introduced himself, and agreed that it was a good idea to correspond via email and meet each year during our visits to Cornwall. This would help him and other group members decide whether I would suit their requirements. In my reply, I included further details of my life, magical experiences, and sent him photographs. We exchanged a few emails in the weeks that followed, and Tony expressed his gratitude for my honest and detailed information. He then revealed more about himself, and explained that he had used a pseudonym for the Pagan email list instead of a real name. Tony informed me his real name was Daphne, and her confidential revelations about her life surprised me. She also told me more about her partner Josephine. Our communication continued.

Two of my Reiki students, June and Emily, requested tuition from me for a magical ritual, so once again, I became part of a working group. After working within a coven, I preferred any group members to work with me as equals. At times, this was rather difficult, as they expected instruction and leadership from a teacher. We all worked well together, and June was particularly good at ritual. She was also one of my best Reiki students. I continued teaching them for a while to see how the group progressed.

As Paul and I had left the Morris team, he announced it was his turn to choose our next family activity, as it was originally my idea to join the Morris team. We joined a mediaeval longbow archery group who wore authentic attire and performed at historical events. We became active participants at the Battle of Camlann re-enactment in Tintagel with the other archers and soldiers. Paul and I enjoyed this pursuit, although I would have preferred an activity that included dance, but felt it was fair to agree with what Paul wanted this time. Teaching Reiki courses and providing healing treatments kept me busy, but the work is irregular. Paul assumed the 'Reiki phase' would eventually die out due to scepticism, and this opinion was supported by his mother May. They did not view holistic therapies as a 'real' occupation, even though it had successfully helped many clients with their ailments and emotional problems.

I continued to attend the mediumship development circle hosted by Ernest and Shirley, the couple I met at the Scole seminar in Norfolk. Shirley would meditate and gradually fall deeper into a trance state. I witnessed various stages of her 'letting go' and giving access of her body to spirit energy. She often connected with an Indian Chief spirit guide who appeared so suddenly with a loud gruff voice and startled group members. Before her trance, Shirley would loosen her clothing and undo her brassiere, as her body took on the physical attributes of the Indian Chief, along with his character. They taught me preparation of mind and body for deep trance meditation, and I was rather hesitant about giving the spirits control, especially when I sensed them near me. I asked the spirit to step back on a few occasions, as I did not feel ready, however when I became more accustomed to this feeling and relaxed, the connection was a slow, gentle process, producing a wonderful euphoric feeling. In the past, I was put off by a certain television programme where Derek Acorah, a spirit medium, would 'overact' his sinister deep trance connections within various haunted locations. He exaggerated spirit possession in a negative way with an uncontrollable outcome, so I was relieved to discover this was a false representation.

I celebrated Autumn Equinox with June and Emily, using a copy of a ritual Sally had performed within the Gardnerian group. Emily, the youngest student, giggled constantly throughout the ritual, and I assumed this reaction may have been either anxiety or excitement. During the summer, Emily asked Paul and I if she could join us for a few days during our Cornwall vacation. Although Emily was in her early twenties, she acted much younger, and we were surprised that she was so forward in requesting this, as we had known her for only a short period of time. Emily had developed a close friendship with June, who was married with two sons and openly expressed her regret that she did not have a daughter. June had a motherly energy that Emily responded to as she came across as a 'needy person,' but despite my reservations, I hoped their friendship would be a successful one.

Organising monthly rituals and hosting Reiki 'shares' kept me occupied. However, hosting all meetings and development groups at my home proved to be hard work. Paul did not wish to participate in development circles, but continued with the Reiki I had taught him and was present for our 'shares.' When our magical group met for the Yuletide ritual, it was evident when setting up the space that June and Emily had not practised or remembered anything I taught them, and expected regular prompting. I realised that as long as I was present to teach them, they would remain 'followers.' I decided the only way their work would improve was by continuing their rituals without me. I informed June and Emily that I had taught them enough to continue alone from then on. June did well with this; she sent me photographs of her ritual altars and made a note of the results of her meetings with Emily and Irene.

– St Nectan's Waterfall Meditation Room, sheltering from the rain on Samhain.

– Practising with the Archery Team

# Chapter 14

## Spirit Connection

*October 2004 – January 2005*

I applied for a position as a volunteer visitor at the local nursing home, but to be accepted, the home required a routine Criminal Record Bureau check. This did not bother me, as apart from a speeding ticket, I had no criminal history. I was also married to a policeman and spouses had to conduct themselves accordingly, as their behaviour reflects on their partner's position. When the C.R.B. returned with no past convictions, they allowed me to visit the nursing home. This helped fill a void in my life, as I had no contact with my own parents because of their religious shunning rules. I enjoyed visiting the elderly. However, most of them were unable to converse, as they either slept, or their minds were elsewhere. There were some I could communicate with who had suffered severe strokes and were paralyzed, except for movement of only one arm.

I befriended an elderly man, Archie, who enjoyed playing cards and board games. He spoke of his family and the fascinating war-time adventures he experienced. When his daughter arrived, I left them to their private conversations and conversed with Larry, another elderly man, who was quite deaf from working on gunships during the war. He related experiences of how one ship had been struck by a bomb, and all the crew had jumped into the sea and were floating in the water, waiting to be rescued. Not all of them survived, and Larry told me how some had seen angels with those who were dying. Larry had recurring digestive problems from the huge amount of oil he swallowed from the ship whilst in the sea.

An elderly lady who had dementia was convinced that I was her daughter, and cried with happiness to see me. I did not want to spoil the moment for her, so I went along with it, making general conversation. Another lady had been placed in a separate nursing home from her husband and she missed him. One woman who was quite a character and made an impression on Ruben was Mary. The staff told us she was once a pilot in the war. She was mischievous and well-known for escaping from the home if the doors were unlocked, so she needed constant observation. Another

114

feisty lady, Edie, who also had dementia, seemed to have a strong link with the spirit world, and was regularly visited by her husband's spirit. He was not welcomed by her, as she cursed and shouted "Not you again!! F... off!!!" When I arrived one afternoon, Edie asked me where all the children came from, who apparently ran into the room as I arrived. She rebuked a little boy for upsetting another child, telling him to leave the little girl alone, and commented that she was not surprised the child had died. Edie also asked Ruben if he was the little boy who leapt around the room and disappeared through the wall. The nursing home had once been a wartime hospital, and it would not surprise me if there were many spirits around the property that were seen by the residents. There are those who do not understand dementia, and most nurses view the patients as 'talking nonsense,' but after listening to those affected by it, I have concluded that the mind prematurely enters the spirit world. The body, however, fights to keep it in the physical world, and this struggle continues until they pass over completely. Ruben would play the piano for residents on the occasions he accompanied me, and he very much enjoyed talking to them.

We visited one Christmas when the local Vicar was there. We sang a few seasonal Carols, and then the Vicar led them in prayer. I had brought Larry a small tipple of rum, as I knew he loved it. During the prayer, Larry searched for the rum. Being quite deaf, he did not realise that the Vicar was praying and everyone else was quiet. He eventually found the bottle that the nurse had moved and shouted out, "I thought someone had nicked my bloody rum!!!" Ruben thought this was hilarious!

I visited the nursing home twice a week over a period of eighteen months. One afternoon, when I arrived, a nurse informed me that Archie was unwell, but allowed me to visit him in his room. I sat upon his bed to hold his hand and noticed the laboured sound of his breathing. Although I had not experienced this before, I sensed it may be what is known as the 'death rattle,' where breathing becomes noisier and erratic before death. Archie and I were alone without the presence of nursing staff, so I seized the opportunity to speak to him about the spirit world. Archie informed me that one of his friends had passed away, so I explained that he had entered the spirit world, and would be at a reunion celebration with friends and family who were waiting for him. He hoped I was right, and I assured Archie that when his time came, he would not be alone, as his wife would greet him and show him where to go. He repeated again that he hoped I was right, and I asked him to send me a sign from the spirit world when he arrived. He promised me he would. While talking to him about this, I entered a level of consciousness that was so powerful. I felt such positivity, as though anything was possible. I can only explain it as a type of euphoria mixed with unconditional love. At this moment, a large cluster of lights like diamonds appeared above Archie's head and twinkled at me before disappearing, and I saw smaller lights that appeared around the edge of his bed. The reading light on his bedside table also flashed on and off. I described the spirit lights that I saw, and he had seen for himself the reaction of the bedside lamp. I explained these as signs that those in spirit were listening to us. When the time came to leave him and collect Ruben from school, I gave Archie a hug, but he would not say goodbye, as he did not want me to leave. I left his room and walked along the corridor. I heard him suddenly call out 'Goodbye' to me with all his might and I called back to him. I now regret that I did not return for one last hug.

This visit occurred on a Monday afternoon. The following Friday, I attended a monthly reflexology exchange afternoon with other therapists. I reclined in a chair while receiving a treatment, and a large cluster of lights suddenly appeared from the corner of the room near the ceiling, identical to the one that appeared with Archie. I knew it was another 'spirit light' but did not realise the connection until Saturday, when a nurse called at my home to inform me that Archie had passed away on Thursday. I believe the lights I saw on Friday were the promised sign from Archie to confirm he was now in the spirit world. I have not seen lights in this formation since that day.

It was my wedding anniversary a few days later. When I had mentioned this to Archie he did not want to be reminded of it, because he had a 'crush' on me. I sat in my lounge alone that day reading a book, while Paul was at work and Ruben at school. All was quiet. I heard a gentle 'tap,' and noticed the anniversary card Paul gave me had been knocked down from the windowsill. It had not disturbed any other cards that stood beside it, even though they were close together. This amused me, as I remembered Archie's words. I will always remember him, and I am sure our paths will cross again when my time arrives to enter the spirit world. The extraordinary experiences I had with Archie were a wonderful gift from the spirit world, because I had devoted time to be with him and had grown so fond of him. Members of Archie's family also visited me just after his death to express their appreciation for bringing happiness and light to the last days of his life.

I continued with my solitary magical work and attended Reiki, Yoga, and Aikido martial art classes. I enjoyed the solitude of magical work, as other pursuits involved intense work within groups.

I prepared to construct a black scrying mirror as a new project at the beginning of 2005. This inspiration came from the dark mirror displayed at the Museum of Witchcraft, as it was one of my favourite artefacts. I spent most of my time with it on yearly visits to the Museum. It is easy to enter a trance state when focusing upon it, and the magnetic 'pull' of the mirror is tangible, as one is drawn into this wondrous magical tool and worlds beyond its reflection.

I followed detailed instructions by Kathryn Breene, sent to me by Clive, a lovely elderly man I conversed with via an internet Pagan e-group. I eventually met him in 2003 during a visit to his hometown of Whitby, an intriguing place with legends of Dracula and Gothic events that are held each year. I then purchased a rosewood framed mirror from an antique shop in the town of Sevenoaks, Kent, and removed the original mirror from its frame. Paul thought it a waste as he said the mirror was of good quality. I purchased a piece of glass cut to the same shape as the mirror, and on specific moon phases within a sacred space, I cleansed the glass and applied several coats of black paint. Each coat needed to dry before applying the next when the moon was once again in its full phase. This process took time to complete, but with patience and focused work, I now own an extremely powerful tool for spirit connection.

Before construction of the mirror, I also followed instructions on how to brew a powerful condensing fluid that cleansed the mirror during its creation. After its construction, the fluid would be used to cleanse and infuse the mirror with energy before and after use. As the condensing fluid is toxic, it is stored in a dark labelled bottle at the back of my potion's cupboard. The black mirror has produced impressive results and is an extremely beneficial tool for my work.

– My dark mirror

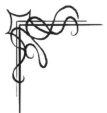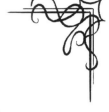

# Chapter 15

# New Introductions

*March 2005 – July 2005*

The Cornwall Pagan Conference changed its venue in 2005 from Camelot Castle Hotel in Tintagel to Penstowe Manor in Bude. They required a larger venue, as the event became more popular and the numbers had grown.

Penstowe Manor was a grand Gothic period property with the right ambiance for this type of event. Chalets were available within the grounds to accommodate attendees who had travelled there for the weekend. Paul and I arranged to attend the first conference at the new venue, and Alexandra (the small confident woman with the crooked top hat) was one of the speakers that year, who told the story of her life and work as a Wisewoman. Alexandra's image was rather unique, compared to other Pagan women, with their flowing crushed velvet dresses and their long cascading hair. Her attire and mannerisms were rather masculine, which caused me to wonder about her sexuality. Alexandra's talk was interesting, with plenty of humour added. On more than one occasion, she cursed and apologised to the audience. However, it continued throughout her talk, and she assured the audience that it was not deliberate. She was one of the regular organisers of the event, and later that afternoon, she stood on stage beside Lana to draw the raffle and announce the winners. Alexandra provided cheeky 'banter,' which Lana tolerated while working with her. She commented on each woman who approached to collect their prize, giving an impression she would not mind 'dating' them. It seemed to amuse the women who were accustomed to Alexandra's 'holiday camp' persona, but Paul was obviously not amused.

During our lunch break, a female photographer from the Cornish Pagan Wheel magazine introduced herself and asked if she could take photographs of me outside the venue. I agreed and followed her out of the building where a group of Gothic Pagans in dramatic attire were outside the manor waiting for her. I recognised Tracey and Laura, as I often danced alongside them during the evening entertainment. Laura was an attractive young French woman who wore a fabulous black leather witch's hat. This hat was a catalyst for various topics of conversation about leather attire and fetish parties. Patrick, the renowned artist, had also expressed a desire to paint my image that day. I appreciated the compliment from someone whose paintings I admired.

I made the mistake of consuming a large glass of red wine rather quickly with my lunch, as it does not take a huge amount to affect me. The first afternoon speaker was a renowned author and Witch, who encouraged the audience to participate in a relaxing meditation. We closed our eyes as instructed and she began to count: "...one...sleeeeeep...two...sleeeeep." As this continued, Ruben, who was now thirteen, saw the funny side of many situations and stifled his laughter as this meditation proceeded. The speaker looked directly at him with a scolding stare. Ruben's laughter was often infectious, and being 'merry' from the effects of the wine made it difficult for me to keep my composure. The next speaker was an archaeologist with an unfortunate 'lisp.' Ruben also found this amusing, but managed to keep his laughter under control. The talk was fascinating, as the speaker had brought a selection of photographic slides, but it went well over the allotted time by at least twenty minutes. The audience began to get restless, and I noticed Alexandra standing at the side of the stage discussing with Lana how they could tactfully bring the talk to a close, as the speaker did not seem to realise. Ruben could stifle his laughter no longer when the speaker with this unfortunate lisp said, "Personally, I find the sacred sites quite fascinating!" I then reacted to Ruben's laughter, and tears ran down my cheeks. The scenario was like something out of a comedy; the talk had run way over time, the organisers were unsure of what to do, the audience was fidgeting, and the speaker had no idea!

We had a wonderful time at this conference and stayed in one of the chalets. The rooms, however, were cold and damp in March, as they are built for summer vacations. The electric coin metre needed to be regularly topped up with coins, much to Paul's annoyance. It was the only time I stayed in one of the chalets, as we arranged day visits for any future events.

While communicating with Daphne from the Craft of the Cornish group, I mentioned that I would be attending this conference. Daphne and Josephine decided not to attend that year, but suggested I introduce myself to Jack, an elderly man who was Priest of the magical group. Daphne explained that he resembled a renowned comedy actor, which made it easier for me to identify him. Jack's colourful waistcoat and ribbons on his hat reminded me of a Morris dancer. He was a lovely friendly man who told me about his group, and then gesticulated toward a woman named Carla. She was also a member of his group, but I did not meet her on this occasion.

Although Jack was an elderly man, he was full of energy, and was also the first person on the dance floor when the lively music began. I danced with him for a while as other people that knew him joined us. This conference was certainly a memorable one!

During May of 2005, I began teaching Reiki courses for Tarran, my Reiki tutor. He had a team of students who were Reiki masters in all areas of the U.K. Tarran provided the manuals and dealt with correspondence. He would send the new students to teachers in their area for the practical aspect of a course. On completion, he would send them certificates signed by him and their course teacher. I taught many Reiki courses for Tarran in the South East area of the U.K.

Paul and I began to search for properties in Cornwall, and I regularly visited our local library to research on the internet. I printed out those that suited our requirements and took them home for Paul to look at. The viewings were arranged on our next visit to Cornwall. The first property was an empty chapel that needed renovation, and I loved its gothic appearance. We later discovered that the graveyard was still in use and had plot reservations for future burials. This could have been rather awkward when planning a summer barbecue, and there was no way we could have a private garden, so we decided not to pursue that one.

My first Reiki students, Emily and June, invited me to join them for ritual work. I arranged to visit their places of residence so that they were in control of preparations and setting up the space. June wanted a third person to be present, as she realised that Emily had developed an infatuation for her. I had experienced this within groups when younger people can occasionally develop intense feelings for an older friend as a 'parent figure.' This can fill a void within their lives, but June felt uncomfortable about it. I attended their rituals for a while until June made the decision to distance herself from Emily.

Tessa, the woman I met at Ernie and Shirley's Reiki shares, booked a day's workshop for us at the London College of Psychic Studies. This event occurred only three days after the Kings Cross bombings in London, and I felt a little apprehensive about using public transport at this time. Paul kindly offered to transport us. The college is a fascinating building with large stone pillars at the entrance, Georgian windows, and spacious rooms. The lifelike portrait paintings of spirit mediums who founded the venue hung on the walls. They seemed so real, that their eyes appeared to follow us around the room. The presence of spirits produced an intense energy within the building. I also spoke to some of the attendees who regularly heard talks and participated in workshops there. I would have loved to attend more events at this venue, but the journey through the busy city of London was a long and difficult one for us. Louise, the friend I met through the Egyptian group, had attended these workshops regularly, as her place of residence was near the venue. I enjoyed our day immensely and hoped that one day in the future, I would have the opportunity to visit this fabulous place again.

May decided to pay me a visit one afternoon while Paul was at work. On her previous visits, I managed to avoid conversing with her at length, finding other chores to do so that I could leave her with Paul. May enjoyed debating, challenging most subjects that were raised. She had made it clear that she did not approve of my beliefs or occupation. I did, however, receive positive feedback on the cleanliness and tidiness of our home, as well as the care of my children. Paul once filmed me bathing Ruben when he was just a few days old, and after viewing it, May thought the video footage good enough to use when training new mothers! This was indeed a compliment coming from a nurse tutor.

I felt rather uncomfortable in her presence that afternoon, since I could not escape or avoid the subjects she raised in conversation. On this occasion however, I was experiencing premenstrual syndrome where I could be more outspoken, so I rose to her challenges. May told me she had no belief in 'life after death' and only believed in things that are proved scientifically. I questioned her frequenting a church that taught its members about a heavenly afterlife. I also pointed out God was not a scientifically-proven entity. May replied that her attendance was more about social-ising. She then added that she did not believe in occult practices, referring to it all as fantasy. Ruben was a spiritual, open-minded child, and when she babysat for him, he talked to her about my beliefs. May told him that spirits did not exist and magic was not real. It upset me that she had said this to Ruben. I told May that she was in no position to judge something she had not experienced or researched. She did not reply to this.

May placed her property on the housing market, explaining to Paul that there were unexplainable occurrences within her home. Objects had moved and then reappeared in unusual places. A buyer made an immediate offer on the property, but changed his mind soon after. May decided that selling the property no longer mattered, as the unusual activities within the home had ceased. She had consulted an optician about these visual disturbances, but her test results were normal. I wondered whether the spirit of Kevin had created a little mischief, as her judgmental nature and scepticism annoyed him. He was a mischievous character and would have enjoyed this role!

We were concerned about May when her home had been burgled. I had studied magical 'thought forms' and learnt more about them in the Alexandrian Coven. To create one, you needed to decide where it would reside, what it would feed on to keep it going, and what its tasks would be. I purchased a photo frame that May would like and set up a ritual to create the thought form. I decided it would live within the photo frame and would feed on daylight, as May had large windows in her home. Its task was to protect May and the home from intruders, and would remain active until she eventually moved. I then placed a family photo of Paul, Ruben, and I in the frame, and gave it to her as a gift. May, pleased with it, placed the frame on her cabinet in the lounge.

Although our family life was exceptionally active, I often thought about our next visit to Cornwall. During the next vacation there, exciting developments were about to take place!

– Penstowe Manor, Bude Pagan Conference 2005

– The converted Chapel on the property market.

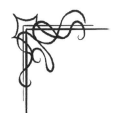

# Chapter 16
## Exploring New Realms

*July 2005 – March 2006*

Our next visit to Cornwall was another eventful one. We arranged our first meeting with Daphne from the Craft of the Cornish group after we had conversed via email for some time. Daphne and Josephine suggested we meet by the promenade near their place of residence. They included photographs so that we could identify them, and as they were very tall with bright blonde hair, it would not be a difficult task. We walked along the promenade and past the skateboard park, where a young boy lost control of his skateboard, which hit my ankle. We sat upon a wall opposite the skate park until Daphne and Josephine appeared in the distance walking towards us. Paul and I greeted them both with a kiss on the cheek, and we sat on the wall to have our conversation. They obviously felt comfortable with us, because they eventually invited us to their apartment in a grand period property that had spacious rooms.

We discovered Daphne had creative talents and were shown some of her work. Josephine told us she was neither interested nor involved in Paganism, but had good business and promotional skills, finding ways of marketing Daphne's talents. During our conversation on business ventures, Josephine mentioned that modelling websites could be lucrative by corresponding with male clientele. Daphne corresponded well by email, but when meeting in person, was rather quiet and said less than I expected. Although we heard that Daphne was born and raised in Kent like myself, Josephine controlled most of the conversation and seemed to be the dominant person within their relationship. When Daphne relaxed and conversed a little more, I heard more about her magical relationship with Jack, the elderly man I met at the conference. Daphne told us of her decision to leave Jack's magical group, as he did not agree with her future plans and life choices. This was disappointing, since Daphne had been part of the group I hoped to join, but she explained her plans to set up another group. We seemed to get on well, so we arranged for them to join us at the Battle of Camlann re-enactment. Our first meeting with Daphne and Josephine seemed to be successful, and so our communication continued.

On our return, I excitedly told June and Emily about our wonderful vacation. As well as being my Reiki students, I had also taught them magical ritual work, so they could understand my love of Cornwall. They planned to join us for a few days on our next vacation there. Emily brought her two-man tent, excited about sharing it with June. June felt uncomfortable about this arrangement, because of the 'crush' Emily had developed towards her. The static caravan we hired had plenty of room, so I offered June accommodation on one of the 'fold-out' settees. This upset Emily, as she did not wish to stay in her tent alone, and asked if she could also stay in the caravan. We assured her that she would be safe in her tent, since many families surrounded her in the campsite. Monty, a member of our archery group, had visited Cornwall to join in the battle. He was a single, middle aged man and a caregiver for his mother who had dementia. My Welsh pen friend Rhonda was also single and a caregiver for her disabled father, so I put them in contact with one another, as they were in a similar situation. I hoped they would communicate for some time before arranging to meet, but only two months after corresponding, Monty announced Rhonda had arranged to visit him and stay at his home. This was rather disconcerting, because they did not know one another well, and I discovered that 'matchmaking' friends can have negative repercussions, even when done with good intentions. The Battle of Camlann was enjoyed by all, and Daphne and Josephine met with us once again. All of our friends returned to the caravan to spend the evening with us. It was a new experience for me spending time with such a diverse group of individuals that night! It was also, however, a relief when the weekend was over and Emily, June, and Monty left us to return home. Emily resented staying in her tent alone, and I later heard she visited June's friend Irene at her place of work, tearfully relating her awful weekend. She told Irene that we allegedly forced her to sleep in her tent, but failed to mention that we fed her during her stay and transported her each day to wonderful locations, ensuring that she was safe.

A beautiful period cottage by the name of St. Pirans was situated on the path leading to St. Nectan's Glen in Tintagel, and on this vacation, we discovered it was on the property market. Paul and I had often conversed with the elderly couple who owned it when visiting the Glen, as they advertised various 'bric a brac' items for sale within the cottage. They had recently passed away, hence the reason for the sale. Paul discovered the garden gate was open, so we entered to look around. We met another family who had the same idea. They were peering through the empty cottage windows and discovered one was open, so they climbed into the cottage and we followed. It was a 16th century property, and the floorboards in the bedrooms bowed at the centre. The stone steps on a small staircase were steep and well-worn.

When I entered the kitchen, I felt a distinct cool energy of spirit presence, and was certain the elderly couple were still there. I discussed this with the other family, who also believed in the world of spirit and had their own experiences to relate. I loved the cottage dearly, but it was well out of our price range at £500,000. I thought about it often after our return. A week later, I entered the occult shop in my local town, and Irene, who worked there, informed me a customer visited the shop and mentioned she had purchased St. Pirans cottage. It was an astounding coincidence that someone living so local would be the new owner. How fortunate she was!

I spent time contemplating my developing friendship with Daphne, as I wondered whether her chosen life changes would affect our friendship. My main concern was if she would feel resentment towards me, for reasons I cannot in all good faith go into. I voiced my concerns to Paul, and he replied by saying that the only way I would find out is to take a chance and see how things developed.

Paul and I eventually left the archery group, as we could no longer afford to continue paying the high insurance fee. Monty, the archer who attended the Battle of Camlann, had behaved inappropriately with Rhonda during her stay, and he also spread false rumours about us to her and other members of the archery team. Rhonda ceased communication with me after seven years of correspondence over this. I have discovered throughout my spiritual journey that the spreading of false rumours has occurred on numerous occasions, and it has mainly involved 'friendships' with ineffectual men.

The time had arrived for me to move on from Ernest and Shirley's deep trance mediumship circle, since new members had joined and changed the group dynamic. This also interfered with the level of our work, as beginners had to be taught. Shortly after leaving, I discovered another new psychic group nearer to my home. Shaun, who hosted the circle, was a spirit medium with a disability resulting from a serious accident at work. He fell from a scaffold and broke his back only six weeks after marrying his wife, Sadie. His disability was the reason he avoided anything to do with Reiki healing, as he thought the energy should have protected him from the accident. I attempted to explain that Reiki does not interfere with lessons in life, but is there to help us through these lessons. This explanation did not alter his opinion.

I discovered that the martial art of Aikido has a strong association with Reiki. Ueshiba and Usui, founders of Aikido and Reiki respectively, were friends;

they exchanged spiritual ideas and practices, so there were similarities connecting both of them. Aikido is more than the use of physical strength toward an opponent. It is mostly about the power of one's mind. I had read a book entitled Complete Aikido - Aikido Kyohan - the Definitive Guide to the Way of Harmony, where a student relates how he met Ueshiba and his experiences there. Uehsiba's senses were heightened to the extent that he could hear a beetle and reach behind him to retrieve it without seeing its position on the ground. While sparring, he could paralyse a person by placing one finger on the opponent's forehead. I learnt how wrist and finger locking techniques can give one total control over an opponent, and experienced how a small female could utilise certain techniques to bring down a male over six feet tall! I enjoyed these classes, and was also impressed by the fitness of my seventy-five-year-old instructor.

On one occasion, while going about my daily chores, I received psychic messages suggesting that I search my husband's jacket pockets. This is something I would not do unless I checked them before loading laundry into the machine. I ignored this suggestion for a few days, but when it persisted, I thought there may be a good reason to do so. I discovered receipts for petrol and cigarettes, which concerned me, as Paul had given me the impression he had successfully stopped smoking five years ago after the death of his father. I discussed this matter with him when he arrived home, and suggested he visit our Doctor to inquire about smoker's support groups. The Doctor gave him a medical check-up during the appointment, where a serious problem was discovered that needed further investigation to identify the cause. The result was severely high blood pressure, and regular medication was needed. This confirmed there was good reason to act upon psychic messages, as they had prevented Paul from going on to develop strokes and other heart related problems. I no longer ignore messages I receive and act upon them, even when they are disbelieved by some until proved otherwise. It is vitally important to trust one's intuition and spiritual guidance.

June and Emily visited me for their second-degree Reiki course. I also invited Tammy on this course, because I thought the energy would benefit her and give her the option of further spiritual development. It is not a Reiki teacher's right to judge whether a person is suitable to learn Reiki or become a practitioner, as all should be given the opportunity to learn. If students are committed to include Reiki in their lives, it will work well for them, but if they decide not to work regularly with it, the energy will move on to those who are. My regular practice of meditation, self-treatments, and empowerments have enhanced all aspects of my work and the courses I teach.

In 2006, we placed our Kent home on the property market and arranged to view a property while in Cornwall. It was a beautiful, converted chapel that stood at an ancient crossroads near Bude. The small garden's patio was adjacent to a graveyard, and across the surrounding fields was a distant sea view. Paul and I loved this property, and we were delighted when we received an offer on our own property six hours after it was advertised. We informed the owner that we may be able to purchase the Chapel soon, but our buyer had wanted to purchase another property that was withdrawn from the market. He used the offer on our home as a bargaining tool to obtain the other one. The owners then agreed to sell to him their property, and he withdrew his offer. Meanwhile, another buyer made an offer on the chapel, so unfortunately, this property was not meant to be ours, and our search continued.

We attended the Devon and Cornwall Pagan Conference in March 2006. Our friends Louise and Leonard attended this event, along with Giles, a mutual friend. Giles attended Leonard's London Occult Group meetings and was also an avid fan of our former Morris team. We knew him from Pagan events and our past performances. The entertainment for the Friday evening before the conference was a folk singer, who performed his music in the lounge bar. Leonard frequently left our group to visit his chalet, and I discovered from Louise that he was still communicating with members of Rockbone. Leonard hoped by remaining in contact, he would receive some reimbursement of the money he gave them from the sale of his property.

Leonard had since joined another Coven in Devon, and introduced us to his priestess at the conference. I remembered her from the Nordic group, who performed the closing ritual at the first Pagan Seminar we attended. Louise told me how Leonard would travel all the way from London to Devon for coven rituals, and if he arrived late he would receive a scourging from the priestess. Leonard willingly accepted this as 'karma' for mistakes he had made in past lives. The priestess wore fetish attire to the event, and her husband's black t-shirt displayed the word 'Master.' They spoke openly about their 'submissive-dominant' lifestyle, and although the female was his leader in the role of priestess within her coven, it was obvious she was under the strict control of her husband within their relationship.

On the day of the conference, the theme for their yearly competition was to dress as a favourite Deity. This one proved to be popular, as there were many entrants who participated. I created a Sekhmet costume, and Paul assisted in constructing a headdress with a golden sun disc and a serpent at the centre. The ears of a lioness were attached to a thick headband. I wore a long satin crimson nightdress for her gown, and Louise offered me a large golden ankh engraved with Egyptian symbols to hold. I applied face paint while listening to talks, and as a Leo with feline features, it was not difficult to create the image.

Patrick (the artist) observed me, and on reflection, I regret not asking him to apply the paint for me. When it was time for the competition to begin, all contestants formed a line by the stage, where we then individually stood centre-stage to be interviewed by renowned Pagan Rolf Hemming, or Alexandra, who were the compares that evening. I hoped Alexandra would be the one to interview me, but when a dark Egyptian goddess approached her, she stepped back and passed me on to Rolf. Alexandra commented that she could deal with this one, while chuckling to herself.

The entrant who made the biggest impression was a long-haired man dressed as Cernunnos, as he wore only a tiny pair of pants covered in leaves, along with a small pair of horns on his head. The audience roared with laughter as he cheekily sidled onto the stage, and the compares found it difficult to interview him without laughing. It was obvious that he would be the winner, especially as the judging was decided by the audience's reaction. The conference then ended with a closing ritual. Rolf, a Priest of the Golden Dawn tradition, requested audience participation in the Lesser Banishing Ritual of the Pentagram. This method of setting up a sacred space fascinated me, and the chants were powerful and evocative. The presence of four archangels at the quarterly directions were indeed powerful, and Rolf encouraged the audience to chant and raise energy. The temperature rose considerably in the venue. I was still wearing my Sekhmet costume at this point; this had an empowering effect upon me, and enhanced my personal experience of this ritual.

When it was time for the evening entertainment, I sat at a table with our group of friends in the large hall. We conversed and indulged in alcoholic beverages while awaiting livelier music. I then invited Leonard's priestess to join me on the dance floor. It was not long then before Jack, the elderly Priest of the Cornish group, joined us, spritely as ever. When the priestess and I returned to our table, I noticed her husband was upset. She explained that she had danced without his permission, and this incident turned into a serious private discussion between them.

I left them alone to resolve the matter. Later that evening, Leonard and Louise joined me on the dance floor, along with Giles. I was extremely happy and having a wonderful time with friends. The throbbing beat of the music and the spirit of the dance once again possessed my body, and as I let it take me over, I was unaware someone was watching me from a distance. Alexandra suddenly appeared beside me, dancing and smiling. She seemed more friendly towards me, making appreciative sounds and gestures while watching my movements. I then 'turned up the heat,' and she flirtatiously responded. Other women at these conferences enjoyed regular playful attention from Alexandra, and I could see why. There was momentary body contact instigated by her as we danced, and she then disappeared from the dance floor. I did not see her for the rest of the evening.

During our journey home the following day, I thought about Alexandra. Until our recent encounter on the dance floor, she seemed to avoid me, and I sensed it was intentional. She was extremely affectionate towards other women, but gave me the impression she disliked me for some reason. I was delighted that our recent encounter proved otherwise. I had heard that she often 'charmed' women on the dance floor at
these events, and if she repeated this again with me at the next conference, I would be ready for her!

– Lamorna Woodland

– Converted Chapel in
Poundstock Bude

– Pagan Conference
Deity Competition

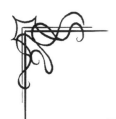
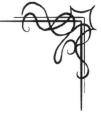

# Chapter 17
## A Lammas Prayer

*June 2006 – September 2006*

I continued attending the magical group hosted by June, and her close friend Irene also joined us for a few weeks. She struggled with feelings of guilt, as she was strongly influenced by her mother's Catholic beliefs. Emily had left the group and was rather distressed about the end of her friendship with June. She contacted me about this, and I explained to her that people enter our lives for various reasons. Some relationships last, while others do not, but each connection will teach us important lessons. I reminded Emily that the magical group is often a temporary arrangement to assist with each members' development. Soon after this, June had a sudden family crisis, which meant she could no longer continue working in the group. Irene, after hearing this, did not want to continue without her. The group then decidedly closed. I hoped their training would help them become stronger women, as there had been times when they were involved in disagreements with others and I had been their 'spokesperson.' This resulted in negativity from other parties directed at me as their messenger. I then distanced myself from their problems and hoped they would learn to resolve them.

It was July 2006 when Paul and I eventually sold our property in Kent and rented another while continuing our search in Cornwall. Preston, a work colleague of Paul's, had advertised his parent's home for rent. His mother recently passed away, and his father was transferred to a residential nursing home. Preston offered Paul a discount on the rent, and after viewing the property, we arranged to move in after our August vacation in Cornwall. I joined two more Cornish Pagan e-list groups on the internet in order to network with the local Cornish community. Daphne was an administrator for both groups, and used three different pseudonyms and email addresses. This caused some members to think the pseudonyms were three siblings rather than one person, as they all had the same surname. On reflection, this was an ideal way for Daphne's introduction to the group after certain changes in her life, as others may believe she had a 'magical family' and lineage.

I reconnected with Gavin, a childhood friend who lived in Cornwall. I first met him when my family attended religious meetings in Fowey. I had known him from eight years of age through to sixteen, and during this time, we were childhood sweethearts. It continued as a 'holiday romance' throughout our teenage years, and at the age of sixteen, we both left our parent's religion and led different lives. I had recently found Gavin's profile on a reunion website and discovered he married at eighteen and had four children. Paul and I arranged to meet him and his family during our vacation, and contacted many estate agents to view eight period properties.

Daphne and Josephine invited us to their local moot ritual for Lammas at Sancreed during our 2006 vacation. The village of Sancreed is a stunning place with a beautiful ancient church. We were informed that the field behind the church would be the venue, and it was a hot, sunny day. I observed Daphne as she confidently walked around the field wearing only two large chiffon scarves, one around her new breasts and the other around the hips. It was obvious she enjoyed displaying her body, but unfortunately, Josephine heard one of the men at the ritual commenting that Daphne did not have the correct attributes to take on the role of Goddess and this upset them.

An abundance of corn was piled high within the circle for group members to create corn dolls. We all placed our creations in the centre of the circle for blessing, while we made personal requests to the gods. I asked them for assistance in finding the right property and Paul did the same. I hoped Alexandra would attend, as I heard she occasionally made an appearance at the West Cornwall moots, but Josephine explained that she had other commitments. Paul and I were introduced to the organisers of the moot rituals. Sandra was a plump middle-aged woman with a wealth of long honey-blonde hair and her husband Donald was also rather plump with an unruly grey beard. His image reminded me of a garden gnome, and I soon discovered this was a common image for men within the west of Cornwall. I hugged Sandra on meeting her, and then glanced over at Daphne, who observed this and 'rolled' her eyes heavenwards. I was unsure what had caused this reaction, but continued my conversation with Sandra. The ritual group were welcoming, friendly, and shared their refreshments with us after the ritual.

The following day we visited St. Nectan's waterfall, and I communicated with the spirits there, expressing my desire to find a property. As I did so, I saw a large stone at my feet in the water, covered in red oxide. I loved the 'blood' stones and sensed it would add extra energy to our plans, so I thanked the spirits and took it with me.

Viewing eight properties was rather exhausting, and many of them were not what they appeared to be in the advertisements. Tintagel was an area of preference for me, but as Ruben would be attending Truro college after our move, Paul decided it was better to live in a central location. We viewed properties near Newquay, and although one was presentable, I did not sense a welcoming energy from it. We viewed the last property and then returned to the caravan. I found a free local newspaper and browsed the property section to see if there were any others we could view. I then discovered a beautiful white cob cottage that was described as one of the oldest buildings in the area. We arranged a viewing, and as we stopped outside the cottage, I noticed a black iron witch attached to the wall. I became very excited, because there was also a sign displaying the name of 'Pendle Cottage.'

Penny, the owner, was a lovely lady with a peaceful energy about her. She told us she had purchased this property on three separate occasions, as she still felt a deep connection with it. Penny explained the renovation work that she had done over the years, and we browsed three photograph albums of the process. Pendle Cottage was exceptionally clean, with tiled floors and three inglenook fireplaces. Two of them were at either end of the lounge and one was still a working fireplace. The other had been sealed and contained a bookcase. The third fireplace was in the dining room and had a fascinating clome oven built into the side wall, which was also sealed. The hearth contained an electric heater resembling a small wood burning stove. The floor was below ground level, which provided extra height to the rooms, and all the wooden beams were original ones from ships.

Paul was pleased the property had mains drainage as he was reluctant to maintain a septic tank. The property had three good size bedrooms and an overall colour scheme of white walls and black beams with a narrow 'galley' kitchen extension that was erected during the 1980s. Pendle Cottage was built in 1750, and was reported to be one of the oldest buildings in the area. I immediately fell in love with it and thought it rather auspicious that we found it on the full moon phase, three days after Lammas.

Paul had instructed me to show no emotion when viewing properties, as it would interfere with his 'bargaining power' on the price. It was difficult to contain my excitement about Pendle Cottage. Paul was reluctant to purchase a property so soon after selling our home, however, and he had planned to leave the money in a high interest bank account for a while. I reminded him that after our search, it was obvious that properties in such good condition were few. Ruben was not enthusiastic about the property either, as the ceilings and beams were low, particularly on the staircase. He commented that he would need to wear a 'motorcycle crash helmet' to live there.

On our return to the caravan, Paul contacted the estate agent and offered a sum £11,000 below the asking price. I could see how much effort and care Penny had contributed to the property and was rather saddened by this, but I tried to distance myself emotionally from the purchase and trust in the 'powers that be.' If it was meant to be ours, then they would see to it.

We were invited to a barbecue at the home of my childhood friend Gavin. It surprised me to see that although he left the religion many years ago, he still lived his life as though he were part of it. I conversed with his wife Miriam, who also had family members that were in this religion. I sensed that her marriage was not a happy one. I had fantasised about moving to Cornwall and marrying Gavin in my teenage years, but hearing that he was not the 'ideal husband,' put any 'what if' thoughts to rest! Gavin's sister Louise had returned to the religion after I visited her in 1985. Their parents were still members, and it was obvious their beliefs still had a huge effect on him. I have met many former members who continue to be deeply affected in this way.

After an eventful vacation in Cornwall, we returned to Kent and moved to the rented property at the start of September 2006. We experienced immediate paranormal occurrences from the spirit presence of Preston's mother. On our first evening, Ruben and I were in the lounge taking a break from unpacking and watching a television programme. At that point, we heard a sound coming from the dining room. As we turned to see where the sound originated from, we saw the drawer of our filing cabinet open and then close. Paul called to me from the bedroom where he had been assembling our bed. He explained he heard a sound coming from a large cardboard box behind him and turned to see the top of the box open. It was as if someone had looked inside it before the cardboard flaps were pushed down to close the box again. They seemed to be curious, but did not seem restless or unhappy about us moving in. Preston was her only son, and the spirit of his mother seemed to connect with Ruben, as he often felt her presence in his room, especially while playing his piano.

The property was situated on a busy crossroads near to the local hospital, so nights there were noisy with constant traffic and sirens. Our neighbours occupied the back bedrooms to avoid the noise, but we were unable to do so, since Ruben slept there. Our former home was in a quiet area, and it took us quite a while to become accustomed to living next to a busy crossroads.

After settling in, Daphne and Josephine visited us and stayed for two nights, as they had appointments in London. I suggested that Daphne tried a career in fashion modelling with Versace, so Josephine had arranged an interview for her. Daphne then decided that it was not the career for her. They slept upon an air bed in our open-plan lounge/diner, and Daphne told us she heard objects moving around in the kitchen at night. Josephine was sleeping when this occurred, which was just as well, as Daphne said it would have made her nervous. The rent we paid for the property each month contributed to the care of Preston's father in the nursing home, so we sensed his mother would approve of this arrangement. We occupied this property for two years while we planned for our eventual move to Cornwall. Ruben would have completed his school education by then. It was an exciting time.

– Corn Dollies – Photo by John Isaac

– Pendle Cottage in Indian Queens

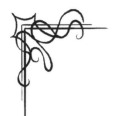
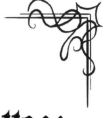

# Chapter 18
## Our New Cornish Cottage

*January 2007 – May 2008*

I had researched Cornish ways of the Craft before my move to Cornwall. During my studies, I discovered a book entitled West Country Wicca - A Journal of the Old Religion by Rhiannon Ryall. In recent years, I have heard mixed reviews on its authenticity, but at this time, I found it helpful to understand the seasonal celebrations in the West Country. I had already researched Cornish words and phrases to include the local dialect within magical rituals. I discovered Cornish lessons for Kernewek Kemmyn on the internet. I conversed with Adam, a knowledgeable man who informed me there were three versions of the Cornish language. Apparently Kernewek Kemmyn is accepted by most of the community. Through this and other discussions, I realised that life in Cornwall was far from straightforward, with many differing opinions on Cornish history, folklore, and religion. The second book I found useful was entitled Hearth Witch by Anna Franklin. It contains seasonal recipes and information on Sabbat feasts, so this book was also used frequently.

Paul and I received the wonderful news that Penny, the owner of Pendle Cottage, accepted our offer on the property at £9000 below the asking price! She was still in the process of searching for another property, and as we were in no hurry for completion of sale, it was a good bargaining tool for Paul, allowing time for her to do so. Although we were extremely excited about the purchase, we kept this news to ourselves until the completion of the sale.

Ernest and Shirley, whose Reiki shares I attended, had planned to move to Wales. I had developed a good friendship with them over the years and would miss my visits there. They told me a few of their friendships had fallen by the wayside, as jealousy occasionally surfaces when a person has the courage to leave their 'comfort zone' and follow their dreams. I visited them on the day of their move to say goodbye while they awaited the arrival of their removal van, which was late due to traffic problems. Ernest and Shirley had eighty cardboard boxes filled with personal items stacked in the garage and in their house. Our move to Cornwall was still eighteen months away, which seemed like an eternity. Ernest and Shirley settled into their new Welsh home and quickly involved themselves with their local spiritualist community. I kept in regular contact with them to see how they were faring.

I researched the location of spiritualist churches in Cornwall, and conversed with a man by telephone who attended the Little Church in St. Austell. I inquired about the healing treatments they provided within the church, and discovered that healers could only participate if they completed the church's healing course. It has an active community, hosting many events throughout the week. He described it as the 'Mother Church' of Cornwall's spiritualist churches. I was pleased to discover that this one would be nearest to my place of residence.

Although I attained qualifications in Reiki, the Japanese method of healing, spiritual healing also interested me. I arranged to attend a course provided by the International Church and Healing Fellowship in Kent. June and her friend Irene also attended this course, although Irene did so out of curiosity. It was hosted by Karen and her husband, who had a severe disability. There were ten students in the group at different levels of development. During the first healing session, as Karen observed us, she sensed a strong Egyptian presence connected to me that she originally thought was male. As the treatment progressed, she then realised it was female. I replied that she may have sensed the energy of Sekhmet, as I often worked with her. Karen informed me that during a past life, I held a position linked with Egyptian hierarchy, and June and Irene were the handmaidens who worked for me. Apparently, in this lifetime, it was my turn to serve and assist them in their spiritual development. This may have been correct, as it was the reason we met. I did not agree with all of Karen's revelations, but apart from that, the course seemed to progress well.

The completion of the property sale took six months, and we returned to Cornwall to collect the keys for Pendle Cottage on Imbolc 2007, when the moon was full. Paul was granted the mortgage, because he promised to give the company his substantial lump sum payment on retirement from the police force. I stood in the centre of this beautiful cottage and observed my surroundings. The realisation of purchasing a home in Cornwall after years of dreaming about it was a powerful and emotional moment.

That evening, I performed an Imbolc/Full Moon ritual within the cottage and included a house blessing. I placed a large white goddess figure at its wonderful hearth that I purchased from the 2006 Devon and Cornwall Conference. The energies within the cottage were powerful, and I sensed a peaceful acceptance from the spirit presence within.

As we had purchased Pendle Cottage, we were concerned about being so far away from it while in Kent. Paul fitted a security alarm system connected to our home and mobile telephone devices. When the cottage's alarm was activated, it would also contact us by telephone so that we could disable and reset it with the use of codes. An intercom within the cottage also enabled us to listen for any activity inside it. Modern technology is so useful in these situations! Our Cornish neighbours regularly checked the property and updated us. I found it difficult living in Kent, knowing we had a beautiful cottage in Cornwall. I often gazed at the framed photograph of Pendle Cottage, wishing I was there, and the time leading up to our move passed slowly.

My spiritual healing course in Kent progressed well, although we soon discovered (as one frequently does within a group) certain members had 'overblown egos.' Irene decided not to continue her course, as she felt uncomfortable about some relationships between group members and thought this contaminated the healing energy. I had witnessed unprofessional behaviour there, so I understood Irene's decision. However, June and I continued our courses, but were distant when working with other members. We focused our attention on achieving our qualification.

Paul and I returned to Pendle Cottage during the Easter holidays of March 2007. On each visit, we were able to transfer more of our belongings. We had also arranged to meet Daphne and Josephine at the next Devon and Cornwall Pagan Conference. During our property search, Josephine suggested that we move nearer to them in the west of Cornwall, and although she sent information on various properties, Paul was not keen on the area. Pendle Cottage was only a forty-five-minute journey from both Tintagel and Boscastle, and it was an hour's journey to see Daphne and Josephine. We lived in the middle of Cornwall, which enabled me to visit either end of the county frequently.

On our arrival at the conference, Leanne, one of the organisers, was first to greet us at the door of the main hall. I had been in regular contact with her, as she also arranged the monthly Pagan moot in Bude that we attended the previous year. Leanne was aware we had purchased our cottage, and it was wonderful to hear her say, "Welcome to Cornwall." She asked me to follow her, and as I did so, I noticed she headed in the direction of Alexandra the wisewoman. My heart began to beat faster as Leanne introduced us. Alexandra took my hand and said, "Oh, YOU are Laetitia!" She remembered me from when I conversed with others on the Pagan internet groups. The moment her hand touched mine, I felt a familiar energy. Leanne then introduced Alexandra to Paul, and I studied her as they conversed. I sensed a deeper side to her that was not so abrupt, but loving and caring with an underlying sadness. After a short conversation, she quickly departed, as there was plenty of organising to do that she had to get on with. Daphne and Josephine arrived soon after us and introduced us to a few members of their local community. We enjoyed the day's talks. However, I observed that if certain talks did not interest Daphne, she would return to her chalet until they were over.

When the evening entertainment began, I headed for the dance floor with Tracey and Laura, who were avid 'followers' of the organisers, speakers, entertainers, and any other renowned Pagans they met. They would sit near the stage and gaze admiringly at the speakers and performers during talks and performances. We danced to the tunes of the regular folk singer, encouraging him to keep the music lively, and at the end of each tune we called out for more. Jack, the elderly Priest, joined us along with Daphne and Josephine. Alexandra soon appeared on the dance floor near the stage and remarked on the ladies' 'heaving bosoms,' encouraging them to continue. They seemed to enjoy her attention.

Alexandra then proceeded to dance backwards in my direction. She seemed to enjoy indulging in 'a bit of fun,' so I seized the opportunity to grab her from behind. After a while, she pulled away from me and danced alone, avoiding my smile and gaze. Daphne and Josephine were rather amused by this, and after a while, Alexandra repeated this move. This time, I took hold of her and would not let go. More ladies began to join in and formed a line behind us, so Alexandra found herself at the front of a 'train' of swaying women. She began to feel self-conscious, aware she was being observed by an amused audience, and attempted to pull away. The more she tried, the tighter I held her until she pulled away with such force, I had to let go. As she shot forward, the ladies behind me fell backwards, resembling a line of toppling dominoes. She then disappeared from the dance floor. While travelling home the next day, I reflected on the evening's events. I was a little concerned that I may have gone too far, and hoped that I had not upset her.

We returned to Kent for a few weeks and then travelled to Cornwall at the end of March. On this occasion, I transferred all magical items to Pendle Cottage, leaving only Reiki literature and therapy items, as I was still teaching Reiki courses in

Kent. I took on as much work as possible, as I was not sure if I would be teaching as many courses in Cornwall.

Our next visit was in June 2007. On this occasion, we were invited to a local inn by my childhood friend Gavin and his family. His sister Louise, who was also a childhood friend, had remained a member of my parents' religion. I was reminded by Gavin's wife Miriam that Louise would not converse with me that evening, and had stated that I 'knew the score,' as I had left the religion. This created an awkward atmosphere, so we decided to leave earlier than expected. My friends Ernest and Shirley from Wales visited us in Cornwall, and loved our new cottage. I had purchased a Grandfather clock from an antiques stall at the Royal Cornwall Show. It was the same age as the cottage, in good working order, with a loud chime. I loved it, but Eric commented that he wanted to leave the cottage before midnight! We enjoyed a day together in Tintagel and they updated us on their lives in Wales.

On our return to Kent, I continued with the spiritual healing course. June and I had attended weekly for seven months, so we approached Karen to ask how much longer it would be before we received our qualification. She replied that we had done enough to receive our certificates, since we were already experienced therapists. We discovered on receiving them that the certificates expired yearly, so we needed to renew them by paying for insurance cover by the International Church and Healing Fellowship. We were relieved that we no longer had to travel to this venue and work within a group that we were not completely comfortable with.

It was difficult living in a rented property on a busy crossroads. The constant noise of cars racing on the town's ring road and loud police and ambulance sirens during the night was difficult to sleep through. It reminded me of the occasion when my family visited New York; we travelled on a Pan Am Jumbo Jet to the U.S. when I was ten and stayed in a Union Street apartment in Brooklyn. While there, we heard the continuous sound of sirens throughout the night and local children played in the streets until four in the morning.

While transporting Ruben to school in the morning, I noticed all our main roads were uncharacteristically empty. Police cars were parked in the centre of the dual carriageway, and as I continued, I saw another police car at the next junction. I did not discover the reason for this until later that day, when I heard that an eleven-year-old boy who attended Ruben's school attempted to run across the busy crossroads after the traffic lights had turned red. He may have forgotten that the 'fast track' buses crossed the junction at this point, and a bus hit him dragging his body beneath it, resulting in instant death. Flowers and other tributes were laid at the crossroads, including his favourite football shirt, and these were visible from our lounge window. I witnessed how this tragic occurrence had affected the local community. A friend of mine who knew the female bus driver commented that she was understandably traumatised and haunted by the frightened look on the boy's face as the bus came towards him. My psychic development circle met at our home that evening and we experienced highly intense energies. It seemed the boy's spirit was still at the scene, feeling confused and unsure of what to do. Our group attempted to help him cross over to the world of spirit, and soon after, the energies felt calmer. We hoped that our connection had been successful and he had found the place where he was meant to be.

Ruben and I attended Tae Kwon Do classes from 2006, as I had discovered through research that teenage boys have a testosterone surge at the age of fourteen. This could result in aggression if it is not channelled into an energetic sport. Martial arts also provides discipline, spirituality, fitness, and protection, so I attended these classes with Ruben, and we learnt together. Amusingly, I was the only mother, as the rest of the class were fathers with their sons!

Our next visit to Cornwall occurred in August 2007, where we arranged another evening out with Gavin and Miriam. Unfortunately, their marriage had reached a crisis point, as he still felt confused from his past religious influences, causing dissatisfaction within his marriage. Paul and I tried to give them advice, but eventually they parted. He felt vulnerable during his divorce and soon returned to his parents' religion. He met another woman at the Kingdom Hall, went through the baptism process quickly, and then married her soon after his divorce was finalised. I knew we would have no further contact after this, as he would have to obey the rule of shunning outsiders.

Paul and I became better acquainted with Patrick the artist while attending the Cornwall Conferences and visiting Tintagel each year. We discovered that he had entered into a new relationship with Naomi, who was thirty years younger. Naomi had befriended Patrick after his wife left him, and helped him recover from depression. Patrick owned a large manor house situated on the cliffs of Tintagel, and I enjoyed our visits there. I sat by the window in his lounge looking out over the ocean while Patrick and Paul conversed. Patrick explained that its location may seem glamorous to many, but the winter months were harsh with no shelter from the elements. Naomi was a 'fantasy artist' with a different style of work to Patrick. She often spoke of her academic qualifications and her honours degree, including the letters after her name in all written correspondence.

Paul was rather puzzled why someone who claimed to have such high qualifications would settle for an occupation of a poorly paid artist rather than pursue a lucrative career. Naomi's artwork began to appear in Patrick's shop as part of the display. This annoyed Paul, as he thought she used his popularity to publicise her own work. At one time, Patrick's home was a welcoming place for his visitors and friends. When Naomi moved in, however, she restricted visits and times so that no one 'outstayed their welcome,' and persuaded Patrick to work more frequently in the studio. I understood her reasons for this, as they both worked in their studio at the manor house and needed time alone to do this. A constant stream of unexpected visitors would be distracting. This change however, did not please many of Patrick's friends, and Naomi became rather unpopular.

While staying in Pendle Cottage, we met a female neighbour who introduced herself as a local Councillor. She told us she planned to host a barbecue, inviting the other neighbours so that we could meet them all. I found this rather 'pushy' and declined the offer, as I preferred to meet them individually in our own time. She had a negative opinion of the area, commenting on the supposedly high number of burglaries that she assumed were done by 'white European' individuals. Paul assured her that the crime statistics in Cornwall were a fraction of those in London. Ruben befriended a group of teenage boys in the area who seemed surprised he lived in a cottage that had a reputation for being haunted. During their visits, they were wide-eyed and nervous when entering the cottage. We had no problems there, but were aware of the presence of a guardian spirit. Paul and I were gradually becoming acquainted with other members of the community, so all seemed to be going well.

Meanwhile, in Kent, during September of 2007, we received an unexpected visit from Leonard, our American friend. He announced that he was in a relationship with a young female member of the Rockbone commune and was considering moving permanently to France. Paul and I were surprised and saddened to hear this, as his relationship with Louise had lasted some time. She was understandably upset about it, and I hoped we would all remain friends, which at times can be difficult in these situations. Leonard's return to the commune surprised me after his previous experience. However, this new relationship did not last, as the commune leader controlled all his 'wives,' and Leonard's young woman also 'belonged' to him. Leonard then returned to Louise once again and they continued their relationship. However, Giles, a mutual friend, was not so forgiving. Paul and I did not judge Leonard, as they had an unusual relationship, and we were extremely fond of them both.

I invited Preston, the landlord of our property, to one of our psychic development circles. He was aware of the unusual activity within the house, especially when the burglar alarm activated during the night, despite the fact it was turned off. He told us that this incident had occurred on the second anniversary of his mother's death, and Preston was curious to know if she had any messages for him. During the group meditation, I sensed her spirit enter the room and embrace him. After the meditation, I questioned Preston about his experience, and he replied that he felt his mother hugging him. Other group members provided messages describing his mother's appearance and where she preferred to sit within the lounge. June described the problems his mother had with her legs and her use of a walking stick. All these descriptions were accurate. His mother gave her approval on the rental of her home to pay for her husband's care in the nursing home. All the messages given to Preston that evening were also accurate, and he left smiling and content.

I received an email from Ben and Jill, the owners of St. Nectan's waterfall, informing us they had placed their site on the property market. They hoped it would be purchased by someone who would keep it in its original state.

During our next visit to Cornwall in October 2007, I volunteered to host the end of season Samhain ritual at the waterfall. June and Irene were eager to assist, so I gave them a copy of the words for invocation of the elementals and setting up the circle. They were responsible for libations and the distribution of small onyx crystals as gifts for the visitors. Ivan, a friend of Patrick, offered to assist me. He had recently taken on the image of Merlin, which suited him. We first met Ivan when he worked in Patrick's art shop, and he was an easy person to communicate with, showing genuine concern when his friends had personal problems. He had serious health issues of his own, but still showed compassion for others.

It was quite a challenge transporting the ritual tools down the steep slate steps to the bottom of the waterfall, but fortunately, there were plenty of willing volunteers. June and Irene were nervous about setting up the space and withdrew at the last minute, so I cast the circle and invoked the spirits. When the space was prepared, we were joined by sixty visitors, including Bill and Sybil, who taught Karate and lived a few miles away from our cottage. I originally contacted them to inquire about their classes, as Ruben and I wished to continue with our training. They seemed to be spiritual people, and Bill claimed to have North American Indian ancestry. These images were displayed on their advertisement. When the sacred space was set and the gods invoked, I asked all visitors to drop their 'papers of regrets' into my large cauldron containing many hot charcoals.

The cauldron began to smoke heavily, so I asked Paul to take it out of the circle. As he carried it towards the waterfall, the contents suddenly burst into flames and shocked the visitors. June and Irene assisted in distributing libations and crystals to the visitors, and they did a splendid job. Bill, our Karate teacher, approached me after the ritual to inform me that he saw spirit entities many times in his life, and during the ceremony, he noticed eight cloaked figures in a semi-circle observing us. Sybil thought that Bill had his arm around her during the ritual, but later discovered his arm was by his side. Many people within the circle sensed strong energies and had their own unique experiences.

Ben, the owner of the site, received positive feedback from all visitors. I had not asked for payment for conducting the ritual, even though it included a lot of preparation and hard work. I considered it an honour to do a ritual at the waterfall. When we said farewell to Ben, I was surprised that he did not thank us for the ritual. The spiritual experiences, however, overshadowed any negative occurrences that may have occurred. Before leaving the waterfall, I thanked the ancestors for their assistance, and asked for their help to attract the right type of purchaser for the site.

During November of 2007, I contemplated closing my Kent psychic development circle. Paul was unhappy about June and Irene visiting each week, and made derogatory comments about their intelligence. After giving it some thought, I decided not to close the circle, but to host them less frequently. Paul had no wish to be involved, and because of that, he had to amuse himself elsewhere on those evenings. He stated that after our move to Cornwall, it would be wise to leave behind friendships and associations we had in Kent and to start anew.

It was at this time that I reunited with Joan, an old school friend I found on an internet reunion site. Joan attended my school for only two years, as she stayed in various foster homes. But during her time there, we formed a friendship, as we were both considered different by other pupils. Joan had a thalidomide deformity, and I was raised within a strict religion, reasons that we received playground teasing and name-calling from other pupils. During those two years, Joan and I choreographed a dance, which we successfully performed during the interval of our school pantomime.

Many years had passed since then, and I was curious to know how she had managed throughout her life; some people with this disability were not expected to live a long life. The first time Joan visited us, she brought a bottle of wine with her, and we discovered that she had a manic and excitable personality. I heard all about her life and the children she had raised. I admired her accomplishments, despite the difficulties she had with her arm and hand. Joan seemed disappointed when I revealed our plans to move to Cornwall within six months. However, Paul was relieved, as he found her 'manic personality' difficult to cope with; during the evening, she grabbed hold of him to tickle him, and he told me she was rough and it was rather painful.

She was sad about us moving to Cornwall, but after she left, Paul commented that he was relieved we were going, as he did not want her visiting us again. Paul had eighteen months left to work with the police force after our move and made plans to commute from London to Cornwall, working five days of twelve hour shifts and then return to Cornwall for five days at home. Paul and I were rarely apart during our twenty-year marriage, and this would be a testing time for both of us.

We visited Cornwall over the Christmas period and celebrated New Year's Eve 2007 in the town of Newquay. The locals wore fancy dress costumes and visited the town's drinking establishments and nightclubs. People of all ages, some with their families, gathered outside The Central public house at midnight. One family shared their bottle of Prosecco with us after distributing their plastic cups, and there was a good community spirit around us as we enjoyed the celebrations.

Our excitement about moving became more intense at the beginning of 2008 as our moving date was getting closer. In 2007, we had travelled to and from Cornwall on fifteen occasions. I tried to contact Lorna, and surprisingly discovered that she had already moved to Australia without letting me know. Lorna still had my statue of Sekhmet in her possession, and living on the other side of the world, I was unsure whether I would see her or my statue again. There had been times when the thought of moving three hundred miles away from an area I knew so well was rather perturbing, but in comparison to Australia, the distance between Cornwall and Kent did not seem as far.

Ruben studied for his GCSE examinations, and I continued teaching Reiki courses and hosting psychic development circles until the day before our move.

Ruben's 'mock' examination results were good, so we were optimistic that he would receive a good passing grade for his actual examinations. May had assumed that Ruben lacked the intelligence required to pass these, and Ruben was aware of this, but I advised him to ignore the opinions of others and do the best he could. I told him that I would be proud of him no matter the outcome, as I reassured both my children that all that mattered in life was that they worked to the best of their ability and took pride in their achievements.

Paul and I were unable to attend the 2008 Cornwall Conference in March, as we were busy preparing for our move. Coincidentally, our former Morris team were performing at this event, which meant we would miss this too. I frequently thought about the conference that weekend, particularly on Saturday evening, wondering if Alexandra had noticed my absence and found another lively female to dance with. I yearned to move away from the negative energies in Kent, and this caused the first half of 2008 to pass slowly. We returned to Cornwall during the Easter holidays and attended the local Pagan moot. There was also an open ritual, but Wilma, the priestess who offered to transport me to the site, was unable to attend, exhausted from an initiation she conducted on Good Friday's full moon. Instead, I had a personal celebration in Pendle Cottage. On our return to Kent, I arranged for one of the psychic group members to continue the sessions by hosting them at her home, as I hoped the group would continue without me. We held a trial group meeting there, but others in the group were not comfortable with the change of venue and my absence as teacher. Unfortunately, the psychic circle then closed.

May announced that she now had a male companion. She had been seeing him for about three years, but thought it appropriate to wait a while after Kevin's passing before announcing this to her family. Paul and I met him when we visited May's home on a previous occasion, and I liked him, as he reminded me of my father. Paul invited them both to dinner, and I hoped May would behave better towards me in front of her new partner. Unfortunately, as soon as she walked through the door, she commented on how Paul would be working in London after our move, stating that I would be contacting him by telephone every ten minutes, as I would not know his whereabouts! I replied that Paul would also be unaware of my whereabouts, and to this, she did not reply.

Her new partner's presence made no difference to her comments. On reflection, I sense she may have assumed moving to Cornwall was all my idea and that I was taking her son far away from her. I missed the relationship I had with my first mother-in-law, and was rather relieved we would be moving away. Ruben was amusingly horrified that someone his grandmother's age was dating as he shockingly described them as 'practically dead!' I could understand his feelings, as children hate to think about parents having romantic liaisons, let alone grandparents!

A few days later, I heard from a friend that Joan, my first mother-in-law, had recently passed away, as she saw her obituary in the local newspaper. I would have sent flowers to the funeral, but Paul advised against it, as he thought Derek, my first husband, would not view it as a heartfelt gesture. I had no contact with my family at this time (due to religion and other reasons) and I was also unaware that my Aunt Martha, who I was close to during childhood, had passed away in the summer of that year. My mother converted her sister Martha to her religion, so we had not been in contact for many years.

Our moving date was on the twelfth of June 2008. This date was also the seventh anniversary of our Handfasting, as well as the fifty-seventh anniversary of the Fraudulent Mediums Act and witchcraft repeal. This date will always be a memorable one for these reasons, and it felt surreal to think that our next visit to Cornwall would be as residents rather than tourists.

– Imbolc
Ritual and
House Bless-
ing at the
Hearth.

– The cliffs of Tintagel

– The cauldron used for the Samhain ritual at St
Nectans Waterfall

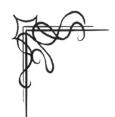

# Chapter 19
## Moving to Cornwall

*May 2008 – June 2008*

Ruben and I attended our local folk festival in May 2008 in order to connect with members of our former Morris team before our move. Six years had passed since our departure from the team, and they did not recognize Ruben immediately; he was a tall teenager now, compared to the small boy they remembered. I conversed with a member of a new Morris team called "Beltane," who were talented musicians and dancers. I heard they were from the South West and hoped that they were based in Cornwall, but it turned out that they were from Devon. Members of our Morris team knew of our plans, since we often spoke about it during our time with them, so they wished us well for the future.

June had invited me to have lunch with her at an Italian restaurant a few days before our move. We had a delicious meal, and she surprised me with gifts from her and Irene for our new home. I knew I would miss June most of all, as we got on well and had been through various stages of spiritual development together. There were also many hilarious moments during our four-year friendship.

Paul, Ruben, and I attended a farewell meal with a group of friends from the London Pagan gatherings. Barry was often a Master of Ceremonies at Pagan events and a lead vocalist with a band. On some occasions, I joined them as backing vocalist, which was fun. His wife Tina accompanied him, as did Giles. I had not seen Giles since he attended the Cornwall Conference in 2006. Claire, a good friend who sang at Pagan events, was also there. We had such a wonderful evening together. It is on occasions like these, that one realises how important genuine friends are.

Paul purchased a transit van for the gradual transportation of furniture during our visits to Cornwall. We accomplished this without any help from friends or family members. On the twelfth of June 2008, while Ruben completed his final GCSE examination at the Grammar school, Paul and I cleared the remaining items from our rented property and cleaned the empty rooms. We collected Ruben from school and then began our final journey home to Cornwall with two vehicles full of our belongings. Paul drove the transit van and I followed him in our family car. During the journey, when I was alone (as Ruben spent time within each vehicle), I had time to contemplate many things. I thought about moving so far away from my family, though I had no contact with any of them at this time.

Five years had passed since I had contact with my parents at my brother's funeral, and even then we did not converse, as they were surrounded by fellow religious members. I had no contact with Tammy either, so my whereabouts did not seem to matter to them. My thoughts then turned to Alexandra the Wisewoman; now that I would be residing in Cornwall, it may provide an opportunity to discover more about her. I sensed getting to know her would be no easy task, as she once explained to me that she had a different outlook on many things to most Pagans, along with a different sense of humour.

The only information I knew about her was from the talk she gave at the conference, and I could not remember most of it, as there were other distractions that afternoon. My idea of what and who a Wisewoman was, was in complete contrast to the image and lifestyle which Alexandra led that did not fit my expectations. I had imagined a 'fairytale' setting of an elderly woman who resides in an old cottage deep within a forest, working solitary and difficult to find.

After six long hours of travelling, we arrived at Pendle Cottage just before ten o'clock in the evening, tired and relieved the final journey was over. Alan, one of our neighbours, was waiting by the gate to welcome us. He had lived in the village of Indian Queens for over eighty years and was extremely fond of Pendle Cottage, relating stories of how he passed it each day on his way to school. Alan was a feisty little Cornish man with mischievous bright blue eyes, and his wife Vera was twenty years his junior, with an interest in running marathons for charity. They were regularly involved in fund-raising for cancer charities, as their previous partners had passed away from this disease. Alan and Vera were a lovely couple and we got on well with them.

I gradually settled in the cottage during the months that followed, but had difficulty adjusting to Paul commuting to and from London. He travelled by motorcycle, which concerned me, since it was such a long and tiring journey. Paul parked his transit van in the car park beneath the police station where he supposedly slept during the eighteen months he worked there. Occasionally, he stayed and cared for his colleagues' properties while they were on vacation. Joan and Irene hinted that it would be easy for him to have an extramarital affair without my knowledge, as he was so far away from home and their words remained in my mind. However, on reflection, I realise this was a projection of their own insecurities. Paul worked twelve hour shifts and his life was extremely busy, so the time passed quickly for him.

Ruben and I began to attend the local karate classes taught by Bill. He was in his seventies, and taught the classes with Sybil, his middle-aged wife. I had hoped to find spiritual teachers who would include this aspect of martial art in their training. Bill had been a military man, and proudly related horrific stories about the time he spent in warring countries. He believed his students should be taught to kill as well as defend, so Ruben and I learnt new and precise karate moves while we were there. After a few months of attending, a young Ukrainian woman joined our class, and it was obvious Bill was attracted to her. She reciprocated and he was flattered, which worried his wife, but this only lasted a few weeks when she realised Bill was not as financially astute as she had hoped.

Ruben achieved excellent examination results and was accepted for further education at Truro College. He seemed excited about his new life, but as we had all been so busy with the move, he did not tell us how much he missed his friends and former life in Kent.

Six weeks after our move, we purchased two kittens from the R.S.P.C.A. We heard that six kittens were rescued from a football pitch after their mother abandoned them, and we visited the kennels to meet them. They had names beginning with the letter F. Flynn was a black male with bright alert eyes, and the fur on his head stood up in spikes. I wanted a black cat, so he was my obvious choice. Paul and I observed the others to find him a companion; two kittens were a beautiful grey colour, as well as a black and white one with the name of Frankie. He charmed us by approaching the glass door, studying us with a cute expression and his head tilted. I renamed them Clutterbuck and Pickingill. When we returned home, Clutterbuck constantly suckled the abdomen of Pickingill, who behaved more like a parent towards him. This activity ceased when they became more independent and explored the outside world.

I received an invitation to a summer solstice ritual with the local moot group. The venue for this ritual was in Saltash, because a member of the group owned land there. I was unfamiliar with this area of Cornwall, so I followed Wilma in her car, who assured me that it was difficult to lose your way when all places were well signposted. The ritual was a wonderful experience. Wilma asked me to read the 'Charge of the Goddess' for them. As I did so, it evoked memories of rituals with my former coven, when Beatrice read this out at all of our rituals. Ruben played the role of the Oak King, who battled with the Holly King to symbolise the changing season. Wilma's high priestess attended this ritual after travelling down from the Northern area of the U.K. Wilma and I got on well together, which surprised her, as she commented that priestesses were usually 'aloof' with one another. I, too, had similar experiences with various priestesses in the past, and Wilma's high priestess was no exception. She looked down her nose at me while firing questions about my training.

I observed Wilma as she set up the sacred space and performed the ritual, enjoying being part of a group without the responsibility of taking the lead. Wilma's high priestess gave me a look that conveyed to me that she assumed I did not like relinquishing control to watch her initiate conduct the ritual. How wrong she was! After the ritual ended, we indulged in a picnic feast, in which I contributed home baked cheese and thyme bread that the group enjoyed. Unfortunately, we had to leave early, as Ruben had a pollen allergy. We had been in the field for some time on a hot, sunny day, and the skin around his eyes began to swell, accompanied by constant sneezing. I thought it wise to remove him from the area, hoping it would relieve his symptoms. The journey home was not as difficult as I thought, as Wilma was right and all the roads were well sign-posted. Our new life and adventures in Cornwall had now begun.

– Beltane Border Morris. Photo John
Isaac

– Karate Classes near Indian Queens

– Our kittens Clutterbuck and Pickingill

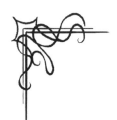
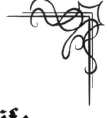

# Chapter 20
## A New Way of Life

*July 2008 – December 2008*

I missed Paul intensely while he commuted to London, though I did resist the urge to contact him by telephone when I recalled May's words, so we did not communicate unless he contacted me. Ruben cultivated new friendships and enjoyed his first summer in Cornwall, visiting beaches of Newquay and learning to surf. I had not met anyone in the village with similar interests or spirituality as myself, so I missed the social activities and friends I left behind in Kent. I arranged to visit them just before Yule. I was extremely grateful to Paul, who turned my life-long dream into reality, and after a period of six weeks, I grew accustomed to his regular commute to London. At the end of July 2008, I received a birthday card from May. For years she had signed it with 'Mum J,' but on this particular occasion, she signed her Christian name. It seemed to be a sign of her distancing herself, although we had never experienced what you would call a close relationship. May had attempted to dissuade Paul from moving to Cornwall by voicing her concerns about the risks of Radon gas. We researched this and discovered that it only reached dangerous levels within a property if it had sealed double-glazed windows and doors with no ventilation. To check this out, we purchased a Radon testing kit for our cottage, and soon found that the levels were safe.

I conducted a solitary full moon ritual during August 2008. I sensed there was a specific reason for moving to Cornwall, as I had experienced the 'calling' throughout my life. I loved Pendle Cottage, but it soon became apparent the area did not have a spiritually-minded community. I began to feel a little disheartened, and during this ritual, I asked the ancestors to reveal the reason they 'called' to me, so that I had a sense of purpose.

The town of Newquay was seven miles away from Indian Queens, and the energy there was rather like a south east seaside town. It was an ideal place for nightlife and parties, as many 'stag' and 'hen' groups celebrate there. It also has 'gentlemen's clubs' that attract some strange characters to the town. My visits there would be quick, purchasing what was needed and leaving as soon as I could. I had attempted to walk around the town and browse the shops on a few occasions, and it was not long before I was followed by unsavoury male characters. As someone who highly enjoys window shopping and taking my time doing so, I did not have the wherewithal this time to linger around the area and pay them any mind.

Ruben's friends were also musicians. They formed a band and practised their music regularly in our garage. They wrote songs and worked hard on their performance. I often visited the garage to listen to them and was impressed by their songs. I transported them to the Tintagel Arms each week and assisted them in setting up their equipment for an evening of 'band music.'

One evening, while Ruben's band practised in the garage, I heard a commotion and glanced out of the lounge window to see them run out of the garage. They stood outside the open doors, staring inside. An object had apparently moved during their practice and startled them. They assumed it was a ghost. One afternoon, when Ruben was studying college work in his bedroom, I heard a loud thud. He explained that he looked up from his desk and saw a dark haired, bearded man in a long dark coat, outside his bedroom at the top of the stairs. The man had been watching him, but then the figure disappeared. I sensed it was the spirit who owned the property back in 1750, who was there as its guardian.

When carrying out domestic chores in the 'galley' kitchen, I often felt a rush of energy from the dining room to the kitchen. I mentioned this to Penny, the previous owner, and she, too, had experienced this. The kitchen was an extension built onto the back of the cottage twenty-five years ago, so the doorway between the dining room and kitchen would have been an outside entrance at one time. During the night, I heard muffled voices and laughter, as if I were sleeping above a busy inn. There were no public drinking houses in the village, and it was unusually quiet at night, given its location. When Paul returned home from work, he drank a small glass of whiskey and felt strangely intoxicated, as if he had consumed much more. He then felt unwell, and we wondered if it may have a connection with the energies and history of the cottage. Its appearance and location on the old crossroads would have made it an ideal place for a 'kiddlywink.' Wikipedia reads: "It was sometimes spelt 'kiddleywink' and is an old name for a Cornish beer shop or beer house. It became popular after the 1830 beer act. They were licensed to sell beer or cider by the Customs and Excise rather than a Magistrate's Licence required by traditional Taverns and Inns. They were reputed to be the haunts of smugglers and often had an unmarked bottle of spirits under the counter."

I received an invitation from Wilma to attend her Coven's open full moon ritual on a lunar eclipse. I travelled to the home of one of her coven members, who resided in a beautiful Georgian property. It had a spacious kitchen with an aga and a wonderful original slate floor. Paul and I previously visited this place for gatherings with the Pagan moot group. The Coven ritual was performed in the lounge. Wilma invited me to invoke the Southern quarter, which worked well with me having a fire birth sign. Her working methods were similar to Alexandrians and the words for the Charge of the Goddess were identical. Blessings for the libations at the end of the ritual were new to me and beautifully evocative. Two female coven members seemed a little reserved towards me; one treated me as though I were a beginner, but this did not matter, as I enjoyed working with Wilma. After the ritual, the partially eclipsed moon appeared from behind a cloud, so we assembled in the garden to admire her.

At the beginning of September 2008, Ruben began his first term at Truro college. At times he felt alone, as many students there had attended school together. There were other students in Ruben's position who had moved to Cornwall from different areas. He apparently experienced some hostility from young Cornish male teenagers, who referred to him as a 'gangster,' because he originated from the London area. Ruben had experienced teasing at his local school and this did not seem to upset him. He began to participate in their jokes dressing like a 'gangster' while attending college.

I applied for work at a beauty treatment salon in Truro. The interview was successful, as my qualifications were compatible with the salon's requirements. I was also trained in the brand of products they specialised in. Fain, the French owner, requested a Reflexology treatment, and he was pleased with my work. On my first working day, I discovered that the journey to work would be a problem, since travelling only twelve miles took an hour with the amount of traffic entering the city at that time. Another annoyance was that the cost of a parking ticket for the day was very expensive. I arrived at the salon on time, but was informed I had to arrive half an hour before the salon opened. Fain welcomed me, introduced me to the other therapist, and then informed us that Shai, his wife and joint owner of the salon, had taken compassionate leave, as she was grieving for her deceased father who passed away a few years ago.

My first day was really busy, as we had no receptionist and were given a brief explanation of how to operate the computer filing system in reception. All payments from clients, their records, and appointments were accessed via a complicated programme on the salon computer. Fortunately, Fain was there to deal with reception duties that day. I was unfamiliar with their latest equipment and there was little time to practise before the clients arrived. On my second working day, Fain informed us he was unwell with a condition known as M.E. and was advised by his doctor to return home. This meant my colleague (who had only been there for one week) and myself were left to run the whole salon that day. The owners had left their business in the hands of two inexperienced therapists.

Shai arrived unexpectedly during the afternoon to witness my unsuccessful attempt of waxing a client's eyebrows using their latest equipment. Shai was a large, formidable South African woman who immediately escorted the client back to the therapy room to repeat the waxing treatment. After the client had left, Shai spoke aggressively to me. I explained the situation, and she reluctantly provided me with a pot of warm wax that I was familiar with. She insisted I used that while practising with their new equipment. I was relieved when she left the salon. It was then that my colleague informed me that many therapists had resigned because of her aggressive attitude. My colleague also spoke of Polly, another therapist who I would meet the following day. She had the same qualifications as myself in holistic therapies. I looked forward to meeting Polly and pleased that we would have another colleague with us who had more experience in the salon. I returned home utterly exhausted and related the day's events to Paul. He was appalled at their way of running a business, as well as the unprofessional treatment of their employees.

On my third working day, I met Polly, and we had long conversations about various therapies, particularly Reiki. She had worked in the salon for four years and kept a collection of crystals in her treatment room to use on clients. Polly knew the salon procedure well, and even though this day was a huge improvement, she revealed further information about Shai and the reasons she had decided to leave. Polly related an incident where she felt unwell and needed to return home, but Shai stood in the doorway to prevent her leaving the premises. I found it daunting to hear about the bullying actions towards employees, and that Polly, the most experienced therapist, had decided to leave. In addition to this, I had also been told by Shai that I would be expected to travel to London for expensive courses in the latest equipment, and would need to fund these myself on a low wage. After everything that occurred and all I heard within the last three days, I decided I could no longer work there, as I did not see the situation improving.

Paul and I received an invitation from Daphne and Josephine to attend an Autumn Equinox celebration in Penzance, their local town. It was the first time the revived 'Harvest Celebration' would take place. We joined the back of the procession, holding flaming torches, and followed the band, while a person led the procession holding a large 'neck' of corn. Josephine captured images of the event. We processed to the Admiral Benbow Inn, which was decorated with colourful antique artefacts from old ships, and we congregated within the upstairs function room. Members of the community had contributed a variety of vegetables to be sold at auction. Dean, a skinny middle-aged man with few teeth, long hair, and a comical personality, led the auction. He made suggestive comments about any phallic shaped vegetables he presented. There were three elderly ladies from the Old Cornwall society, who were giggling like schoolgirls at his antics. I wanted one of the huge radishes, and when Dean held it up, I immediately bid for it, which caused a roar of laughter from the onlookers. Josephine seemed pleased that we were getting along with the local community, and Ruben brought his keyboard along to join in with the music session after the auction. His music was quite different to the folk music the community was accustomed to. Once again, I asked whether Alexandra would join us, and Josephine explained that she had other commitments that weekend.

Daphne and Josephine invited us to their home after the event, and our conversation included Alexandra. Josephine had captured recent photographic images of her, and as she displayed her photographs, she explained that Alexandra was not in a good mood that day. She was reluctant to pose, but agreed after a little persuasion from Josephine. Alexandra looked straight into the camera and her eyes were full of brooding thoughts, which revealed another side to her usual 'social personality.' This intrigued me. Josephine told me that a cloud of smoke appeared in the corner of her cottage, and when she mentioned it, Alexandra replied that she would not be surprised if the smoke was connected to spirit activity. The conversation ended there, as it did not feel appropriate to ask more questions, although I was bursting with curiosity. Josephine updated us on Alexandra preparing a new 'Obby 'Oss for the festival. I had seen the horse's skull on previous visits and gazed at it while they conversed with Paul, unsure of my feelings about it, but intrigued at the same time. Josephine had left the last photograph of Alexandra displayed on her computer. I was constantly drawn to her sky-blue eyes and the messages deep within, hidden from the outside world. I sensed that one would need courage to enter the realms of her hidden personality, and the eventual revelations may come at a price, as many hidden discoveries do.

I frequently visited Tintagel and called to see Patrick and Naomi at their art shop. Naomi announced they had set their wedding date, telling me that Paul and I were invited to their Handfasting on Samhain. Patrick and Naomi were having a midday personal ceremony at St. Nectan's waterfall, attended by a select group of close friends. Later that afternoon, a second Handfasting ceremony took place at King Arthur's Great Halls in Tintagel, where all who were invited had permission to attend. The wedding guests were a varied mix, Naomi's parents and relatives wore formal attire, as if they were attending a church service, and friends of the bride and groom were dressed as fairies, elves, mediaeval re-enactors, and other characters of myth and legend.

It was obvious by her family's expressions and body language that Naomi's life, career, and social life were in complete contrast to their expectations. King Arthur's Halls is a fascinating building, but rather cold, which meant many guests wore coats and cloaks to keep themselves warm during the ceremony. It was conducted by a renowned 'fairie' celebrant who performed the ritual well. The wedding party then stood outside the halls while photographs were taken, and I conversed with Anthea, one of the faerie women. She explained that she was also known by her mystical name of 'Twinkle' during faerie events. Anthea was extremely passionate about her role and believed wholeheartedly that she was a genuine faerie.

After a while, the wedding guests assembled at Tintagel village hall for refreshments. The hall was tiny and could not accommodate all the guests, so they were instructed to help themselves to refreshments and consume them outside the hall. It was fortunately a dry, sunny day, so this was not a problem. Some ignored this, however, and involved themselves in conversation so they could stay inside. Others enjoyed the view of the landscape and were appreciative of the fine weather.

We travelled three miles for the evening wedding celebration at Boscastle village hall, as this was a larger venue. A renowned band performed lively music; Patrick joined them, as he was also a renowned rock guitarist. Ruben met his first serious girlfriend that evening, who travelled from Norfolk, to attend the wedding with her father. Many friends and acquaintances of Patrick and Naomi used their personal skills to contribute something towards their wedding as makeup artists, dressmakers, cake makers, etc. One friend loaned them a horse and cart for transporting the bride. It was a good example of the way a community can pull together and help one another out. This meant Patrick and Naomi were able to have a large wedding without a huge expenditure.

Anthea invited Paul and I to a Faerie Ball in the town of Penzance at The Acorn Theatre. It was the first time I wore a Gothic faerie costume, and although it was fun, it was not something I would enjoy doing on a regular basis. Wearing these clothes reminded me of the times my mother purchased coloured crepe paper to create faerie wings and skirts for my sister and I. This did not fit in with our strict religious upbringing and my mother would have been reproved by elders if they had known. It seemed she had an ongoing internal struggle with her natural magical senses and the religious indoctrination throughout her life. Many people attended the Faerie Ball. There were occasions when I was climbing the narrow winding staircase, that my wings became tangled with other faeries when passing. We needed the assistance of Paul and partners of the other faeries to separate us, which added extra fun to the event.

The following day, after Patrick and Naomi's Handfasting, I had been asked to perform another Samhain ritual at St. Nectan's waterfall to mark the end of the tourist season. Ivan, who dressed as Merlin, had assisted me in last year's ritual and offered to help again. Paul and I arranged to meet him at Camelot Castle Hotel before heading to the waterfall, and as we sat in the lounge bar, Ivan told us he had changed his mind about participating in the Samhain ritual. Apparently, the 'powerful witches' who attended the Handfasting had noticed that the 'sacred space' was not closed correctly at the end of the ceremony. This oversight, in their opinion, allowed negative energies to enter the space. I heard from others that Ivan believed them to be 'powerful witches,' which caused his reluctance to visit the waterfall and assist me. I left the decision to him, but told him I was determined to go ahead with the ritual as planned.

When we arrived at the waterfall, the energy felt wonderful and peaceful to me. Ivan decided to accompany us, but I sensed his anxiety and reassured him that I would cleanse the space with healing energy to balance and settle the area. As I prepared the altar, my candles were constantly blown out by the strong breeze, even though they were placed in deep glass containers. I had lit them on a few occasions, and through my growing agitation, gently asked the spirits for their cooperation; I explained to them that no matter what occurred that evening, I was determined to conduct this ritual. Approximately forty visitors arrived, and although I had prepared a written script for Ivan, we could not read it without candlelight. I decided to discard the notes and perform the ritual intuitively.

I asked each visitor to light a candle of remembrance (and surprisingly, these ones remained alight) and to speak the names of their loved ones in the spirit world. We meditated on the symbolism of the season while connecting with the ancestors, and this was a particularly powerful moment. The ritual was successful, and once again, Barry, the owner, received positive feedback. Ivan was delighted that he decided to participate after all, and I felt blessed to work once again in such a beautiful, spiritual place. There were no negative energies that evening. They were a little mischievous maybe, but nothing appeared to be adversely affected by a circle that was allegedly closed incorrectly.

Living in Indian Queens felt rather lonely at times. An elderly man passed Pendle Cottage each day and noticed my magical charms hanging at the windows and on the front porch. He would pause on the pavement opposite the cottage each morning and chuckle for a while, before continuing his walk. I could not understand why, after all the effort we made to move to Cornwall, the reason for my being here had not yet revealed itself. I continually asked the 'powers that be' to help me understand, but on reflection, I know why the word 'dreckly' is used in Cornwall. Everything here moves at a slower pace.

It was not until late November of 2008 that this situation began to change. I received an unexpected telephone call from Josephine, telling me she had been contemplating while taking a bath and had an idea. She asked if it would interest me to train as a Teazer for an 'Obby 'Oss in their local town of Penzance. Josephine explained how the present Teazer had performed this role for seventeen years, but was close to retirement and needed to train a replacement. She thought that with my Morris dancing experience, Pagan association, and high fitness level, I would be ideal for the role. Josephine explained that I would be required to dance with the 'Obby 'Oss in the streets for certain festivals. As they were folk festivals, it sounded similar to the Morris dancing life that I missed, and it would also involve me in community activities, so I agreed to try it out.

Josephine was pleased and replied that she would inform Alexandra and pass on my details, so she could contact me. I paused for a moment, wondering if I had heard correctly, and asked if she meant THE Alexandra that I met at the Cornwall Conferences. Josephine confirmed this, to which I then voiced my concern that Alexandra may not agree to train me, due to the incident that occurred on the dance floor at the conference. Josephine assured me Alexandra was not upset about it, but I was still unsure. After the telephone conversation ended, I sat quietly reflecting on what had been said. It had been my desire to get to know Alexandra for some time, and in the past, I had attempted to contact her by email, but received no reply. I assumed that it would be difficult to locate her, but it seemed the 'powers that be' had instead brought her to me through Josephine. My next dilemma would be how to handle the telephone call that could occur at any moment!

I was delighted to attend my first 'Friends of the Museum of Witchcraft' A.G.M. on the sixth of December 2008, as I had yearned to attend for many years. Moving to Cornwall had made this possible. It was held at the Wellington Hotel, Boscastle, in a first-floor function room. Ruben and I arrived just after the first talk began, and as it was rather crowded, we found a space upon a large couch at the back of the room. The talk was given by the charming professor on the subject of witch hunts and past executions. He explained the common causes for these, such as petty arguments, scapegoating, and jealousy within a community. The talk highlighted how frequently and easily community members could turn on one another over the smallest of matters that were exaggerated and blown out of proportion.

Ruben enjoyed the talk, as the professor had a way of injecting humour to lighten the serious subject matter. During the lunch break, Ruben and I visited the Museum of Witchcraft, and were rather disappointed to discover it was locked. We stood outside, peering through the windows, until Gary the owner arrived and invited us in. He had a busy schedule, and to our surprise, he left us in the Museum to look around, requesting that we close the door on leaving. It was a wonderful feeling to be trusted in this way, and rather surreal to spend time alone there. The energy was totally different without the busy atmosphere we had experienced on previous visits. There were wonderful occurrences and opportunities presenting themselves, and I was excited about what else the future had in store.

– An offering to the Gods before gathering
a neck of corn. Photo John Isaac

– King Arthur's Halls Tintagel

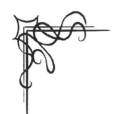
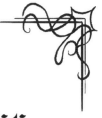

# Chapter 21
## Discovering Local Traditions

*December 2008 – January 2009*

Alexandra was rather shocked when Josephine contacted her and suggested that I train for the role of Teazer. She commented on the emails I had sent to local Pagan e-groups, describing me as a 'fluffy new ager' who was into crystals. Alexandra spoke of my behaviour at the social evenings of Devon and Cornwall Pagan conferences, describing me as a 'blonde party girl' who would not suit the role of Teazer. Josephine asked Alexandra to hear her out, and told her there was another side to my personality that she was unaware of. She explained that I had trained in martial arts and was a former member of a dark feisty Morris team. Alexandra had recently seen this team perform at the conference, so on hearing this, she then agreed to contact me.

I returned from a shopping trip the following day to find a recorded message from Alexandra on our answer machine. I returned her call immediately, and was pleasantly surprised that the conversation we had was relaxed and went on for quite a while. This was a good sign, as Alexandra disliked telephone conversations and usually kept them short. She described the type of personality required for the Teazer role, and I was delighted to hear that being mischievous was important. Alexandra explained how the Teazer role connected with energies of the Bucca elemental, and to see this in action, she invited me to attend the Midwinter Festival on the twentieth of December 2008.

We discussed social activities, as I had assumed Alexandra frequented nightclubs, since I knew she enjoyed dancing at Conferences. I had heard of the nightclub Eclipse in Truro, as Daphne and Josephine occasionally visited the venue. It was one of the very few 'gay' places in the area. I had also visited this nightclub with Paul on one occasion just after our move. I found myself watching the door, hoping Alexandra may appear, but it surprised me to hear that she rarely visited nightclubs. The last time she went there was for her fiftieth birthday celebration.

We conversed comfortably on many subjects, which was a positive sign. She then told me that she had other things to do and ended the conversation. I reflected on our conversation while I unpacked my groceries. I realised Alexandra and I were more alike than I originally thought, as we both had the personality traits required to be Teazers. I updated Paul on our conversation later that day, and although he was unimpressed with the information about the Teazer role, he said that he was pleased I had found a community event to become involved in. Paul agreed to attend the Midwinter Festival with me, but only on the condition that we leave immediately after the performance, as we were travelling to Kent the following day.

On the evening of the Midwinter Festival, we arranged to meet Daphne and Josephine at St. John's Hall. A large crowd gathered outside, and some stood in their positions for the imminent procession. There was a group of teenage female dancers from a local school performing for the crowd that interested Ruben. He wore a black coat, mask, and hat, looking very smart with the right image for the event. I wore a long black velvet coat with a black cat mask. Paul refused to wear 'mock formal' attire, staying in his usual navy blue padded body-warmer, a grey sweatshirt, and faded blue jeans. They looked completely out of place with a black and gold face mask with an attached black tricorn hat!

We stood at the back of the procession, where Paul informed me that Alexandra had arrived. She was at the front of the procession conversing with others. I could only see her battered top hat, as she was much smaller amongst the crowd. Paul suggested I approach her, but at that moment, the procession began to move and gradually made its way through Penzance until it reached the Hill Fort. During this time, I gradually moved to the front so I could observe Alexandra, as she waved to the public and chatted to the men who carried the banner.

The 'Obby 'Oss did not appear in the first procession, so Alexandra had time to enjoy it and exercise her legs at a more leisurely pace. I observed the way she interacted with the community in a slightly different way than she would at a Pagan Conference. She stepped in time to the beat of the drums and I 'fell in step' beside her. She noticed this, but did not realise who I was. When we reached the Hill Fort, I found Paul and Ruben, who happily told me that he had been invited to play his drum with the band in the next procession. We stood beside the beacon bonfire, enjoying its warmth on a crisp, cold evening, when Alexandra suddenly appeared. She conversed with Paul and Ruben and then turned to look at me. I attempted to speak, but the words would not come. Alexandra took a step back, studied me for a moment, then lit her cigarette and walked away.

Paul asked why I did not speak and I could not explain it. In person, she had an unsettling effect on me. I searched the area around the bonfire, hoping to find her and rectify the situation, but she had disappeared. Josephine approached us and introduced her friend Tansy, who was quite a character. We visited a local Inn while Tansy awaited a telephone call, explaining that she attended a Christmas party with work colleagues last evening, and after copious amounts of alcohol, had no memory of what happened. She hoped her friend would remind her and reassure her that she had not done anything she would regret. Josephine and Tansy were conversing with Paul and Ruben, but my thoughts were on the whereabouts of Alexandra. We stayed at the inn for about an hour and then walked back into the town to prepare for the next procession at ten-thirty that evening. I noticed there were more masks worn and darker disguises that could seem bizarre to people who were unaccustomed to this type of festival.

As the procession began, I graduated towards the front. Halfway down the street, the marching band stopped outside a large pair of black and white wooden doors adjacent to an Indian restaurant. The band leader used his large baton to knock loudly upon them, and when the doors did not open, he repeated this. Suddenly, the 'Obby 'Oss dashed out of the doors, followed closely by Alexandra as the crowd cheered. I could immediately see how energetic the role of Teazer was, performing with an 'Obby 'Oss so wild and untethered. The Teazer chased her and I observed her antics with the public. As well as performing moves for the 'Oss to imitate, she gave her signals to snap, laugh, and stand still. The 'Oss rider had restricted vision, so the Teazer guided her along the street and created a pathway within the crowd for the 'Oss to dance through.

When I agreed to train for this role, I assumed being a Teazer would be one performance within the festival amongst many others. I discovered that the Teazer and 'Oss led the procession, and were therefore the main characters and focus of this festival. I grew concerned about taking on this lead role, as it was completely different to the type of performance that I was accustomed to. I knew only three people in this community and the rest of them did not know me, but Josephine reassured me it would all have a positive outcome. Once the Teazer and 'Oss completed their part in the procession, the reluctant 'Oss had to be coaxed into the Barbican, which was her stable. This greatly amused Ruben. After the doors closed behind them, Paul insisted that we leave immediately, so I was unable to speak to Alexandra that evening about the performance. I also missed their celebration as Alexandra, Josephine, and Daphne were delighted with the new 'Oss' first successful appearance. She asked where I was, and Josephine explained that we had a long journey to Kent the following day.

I thought about Alexandra and her performance while travelling to Kent the next day. The mask she wore resembled one worn by the character in my favourite musical 'Phantom of the Opera.' Throughout my life I was attracted to troubled, dark characters, such as the Beast in 'Beauty and the Beast,' Mr. Rochester in 'Jane Eyre,' and Heathcliff in 'Wuthering Heights.' Their traumatic lives, passionate nature, troubled pasts, and darker personalities intrigued me. I wondered why Alexandra had chosen to take on this role, and whether she, too, had another side of her that she kept hidden from the world.

While in Kent, I arranged to meet with June and Irene. They had reserved a table at a restaurant near our accommodation and collected me in a taxi. June invited Josie, her Reiki and magical student. It was obvious she had heard a lot about me on introduction and it was encouraging to see that June was passing on the practices I taught her. June and Irene were concerned about my apparent weight loss and inquired as to whether there were problems within my relationship. I replied that I felt something was not right, but could not identify what it was. I missed being with friends who seemed to genuinely care about my well-being, but in Cornwall, my life was about to undergo dramatic changes. Paul travelled to work in London after spending a few days with us, and something occurred during our visit that made me want to get away as soon as possible. It felt as though I 'flew' back to Cornwall with Ruben and the first time I completed this journey without Paul. The car seemed to have virtual 'wings' and the 'pull' of Cornwall was as strong as ever, so the journey did not seem to take as long.

On my return home, I sent an email to Alexandra, giving feedback on the Midwinter Festival, and surprisingly received a prompt reply. I now had her attention, as we had a mutual interest that she was passionate about. Alexandra arranged to interview me about the Teazer role, but after the exertion of Midwinter she explained that she needed a break and a massage. This meant the interview was postponed until January 2009. I was rather disappointed about waiting a month to see her, but involved myself in other events. I attended a Yuletide ritual hosted by Wilma from the local moot group.

At this event I met Erika, a buxom woman in dramatic Gothic attire. I asked about the local Goth scene and if there were any events approaching. Erika replied that there were no events for mature Goths or the Vampire genre. She told me she once attended a Goth evening at a nightclub and was disappointed to discover she was the oldest one there, surrounded by teenagers. I told Erika about the Vampire New Year's Eve event I attended at the Old London Stone Inn. It was hosted by the London Vampires, who made a concerted effort to impress with their wonderful attire and make up. I later discovered that Jamaica Inn hosted Gothic Halloween events, as Ivan had attended them, but the ticket prices were expensive.

During the Yuletide ritual, Wilma's female dog was 'in season' and very affectionate. Paul had been working hard within the cottage and had not bothered to bathe and change for this event, arriving in his working clothes. The dog was attracted to the odour of dried male sweat on his jeans and she would not leave his side. During the ritual, all moot members stood in a circle for a short meditation. When we eventually opened our eyes, the dog had wrapped her front legs around Paul's leg, attempting to mate with him! The group were highly amused by this and Paul commented that out of all the attractive women in the room, the dog was the only female who approached him!

A basket containing gifts donated by group members was passed around the room. My chosen gift contained small red and green Yuletide candles. Wilma chose a gift containing a quartz crystal bracelet that pleased her, but Erika commented the beads were more likely to be glass than crystal. I updated Wilma on my forthcoming interview with Alexandra about the Teazer role. Although she was unfamiliar with this type of performance, it pleased her to hear I was involving myself in Cornish events. The other Pagans within the group thought West Cornwall was a long way away, and I discovered that even a ten-minute journey was considered quite a trek for some! Paul agreed with them that attending these practices and events regularly would mean travelling forty miles each way from mid to West Cornwall.

All through the Yuletide holidays, it was difficult to focus on our celebrations, as all I could think about was the impending interview. We made sure Pendle Cottage looked fabulous with outside lights and seasonal decorations around all three hearths. We had tastefully furnished the property, including a treatment room in the third bedroom. It seemed nearly all I wished for was given to me, but still...I felt there was something missing.

As we celebrated New Year's Eve and the clock chimed midnight, I did not know exactly what 2009 had in store for me...prepare yourself for the second part of this journey, dear readers, as I step over the threshold into deepest darkest Cornwall in my search for the Old Ways...where I learn that your heart's desire always comes at a price and is not easily attained with obstacles and challenges to overcome. The rewards that await, however, are worth it! The best is yet to come!

**Websites:**
Laetitia Latham-Jones
Village Wisewoman
Crossed Crow Books
The Pagan Federation
Home - Museum of Witchcraft and Magic
Reiki Evolution
The Scole Experiment
Jason Semmens Historian

**Literature:**
Pagan Dawn
Witchcraft - A Beginner's Guide
Hedge Witch: A Guide to Solitary Witchcraft
The Pickingill Papers: The Origin of the Gardnerian Craft
The Triumph of the Moon: A History of Modern Pagan Witchcraft
A Coin for the Ferryman
Fire Child: The Life and Magick of Maxine Sanders
West Country Wicca: A Journal of the Old Religion
The Hearth Witch's Year: Rituals
MASTERING WITCHCRAFT:
Channelling: What it is and how to do it
The Element Encyclopedia of 5000 Spells

Other Titles by Crossed Crow Books

*Travels Through Middle Earth* by Alaric Albertsson
*The Complete Book of Spiritual Astrology* by Per Henrik Gullfoss
*Death's Head: Animal Skulls in Witchcraft* by Blake Malliway
*The Wildwood Way* by Cliff Seruntine
*A Spirit Work Primer* by Naag Loki Shivanath
*Craft of the Hedge Witch* by Geraldine Smythe

Forthcoming Titles

*Celtic Tree Mysteries* by Steve Blamires
*Witchcraft & the Shamanic Journey* by Kenneth Johnson
*Star Magic* by Sandra Kynes
*A Year of Ritual* by Sandra Kynes
*Be Careful What You Wish For* by Laetitia Latham-Jones
*The Way of Four* by Deborah Lipp
*The Magic of the Elements* by Deborah Lipp
*In the Shadow of 13 Moons* by Kimberly Sherman-Cook
*Merlin: Master of Magick* by Gordon Strong
*Tarot Unveiled* by Gordon Strong
*Sun God and Moon Maiden* by Gordon Strong

Crossed Crow Books is always searching for new talent to add to our portfolio of writers. If you have an idea for a book about witchcraft, folklore, magic, divination, mythology, or any other magical subject, we encourage you to reach out to us via our website, www. crossedcrowbooks.com.

Printed in Great Britain
by Amazon

19739400R00105